GROWING AN
EDIBLE LANDSCAPE

GROWING AN
EDIBLE LANDSCAPE

How to Transform Your Outdoor Space into a Food Garden

GARY PILARCHIK OF THE RUSTED GARDEN

CHIARA D'AMORE, PhD, OF THE COMMUNITY ECOLOGY INSTITUTE

COOL
SPRINGS
PRESS

Quarto.com

© 2024 Quarto Publishing Group USA Inc.
Text © 2024 Gary Pilarchik and Chiara D'Amore
Photography © 2024 Gary Pilarchik and Chiara D'Amore, except as noted on page 187

First Published in 2024 by Cool Springs Press, an imprint of The Quarto Group,
100 Cummings Center, Suite 265-D, Beverly, MA 01915, USA.
T (978) 282-9590 F (978) 283-2742

Cool Springs Press titles are also available at discount for retail, wholesale, promotional, and bulk
purchase. For details, contact the Special Sales Manager by email at specialsales@quarto.com or
by mail at The Quarto Group, Attn: Special Sales Manager, 100 Cummings Center, Suite 265-D,
Beverly, MA 01915, USA.

28 27 26 25 24   1 2 3 4 5

ISBN: 978-0-7603-8148-9

Digital edition published in 2024
eISBN: 978-0-7603-8149-6

Library of Congress Cataloging-in-Publication Data available.

Design and Page Layout: Allison Meierding
Front Cover Images: Chiara D'Amore (top left and top center), Shutterstock/JoannaTkaczuk
     (top right); and judywhite/GardenPhotos.com (bottom)
Back Cover Images: Chiara D'Amore (top left and left center), Shutterstock/Arjuna Kodisinghe
     (top right); and Gary Pilarchik (bottom)
Illustration: Trina Dalziel

Printed in China

This book is dedicated to all the people who share our passion and joy for planting gardens, growing food, and sharing the experience with family, friends, and community. Enjoy what you create!

CONTENTS

Gary's yard is a mixture of fruits and veggies, combined with
beautiful flowers. It's a constantly evolving edible landscape.

INTRODUCTION

It's All about Perspective

This book is authored by two passionate and creative gardeners, each of whom approaches the garden from a different yet complementary past and perspective. We thought it would be fitting to start with an introduction from each of us that shares a bit about our journey toward appreciating and cultivating an edible landscape. From there, we'll share more about what you'll find in the pages of this book and how you can use this information to grow a beautiful edible landscape of your own. We hope to help you learn, create, and enjoy.

Adding fall greens and cool-weather crops in pockets of open space through the landscape offers a great way to grow more food in an existing space.

Growing an edible landscape that is both beautiful and productive is one of the greatest gifts you can give to yourself and your family.

A WELCOME FROM CHIARA

Until I was eight, my family moved every year. While houses, schools, and friends changed, the presence of trees, grass, and sky outside each door remained a constant, and nature became my perpetual, true friend. When we settled into my long-term hometown, it was the end of the era when kids were encouraged to go outside and play until it got dark. My relationship with nature evolved into a life-long commitment to caring for the environment. When I was in high school, I earned my Master Gardener certification, and from then on, I planted at least some herbs and vegetables every place I lived—from dorm windowsills to apartments on a one-year lease. I even planted a plot of corn in a rented suburban front yard when I was a young professional commuting to a big city to work for a big company.

The more I "grew up," the less time I spent outside getting my hands dirty and growing things. My love of nature became something I expressed only intellectually through my career. Then I became a mom, and it became important for me to explore and play with my children outdoors and for them to grow up connected with nature. And so I did something wild—I started a non-profit known as the Community Ecology Institute, with a mission to cultivate communities where people and nature thrive together. Through an incredible collaborative effort, we purchased a small suburban farm where we grow food for the community and teach people of all ages and backgrounds how they, too, can grow food. There is nothing sweeter than being at Freetown Farm with my kids and community members starting seeds, planting gardens, and harvesting a rainbow of fresh food. It is so joyful and fulfilling, and it feeds right into my hobbies of foraging for wild foods and making art out of nature.

A WELCOME FROM GARY

My grandfather taught me how to grow tomatoes and other vegetables at a very early age. I saw how seeds grew and how a space that was once part of a lawn could become something magical. With a small handful of seeds, I was able to grow tomatoes, peppers, squash, beans, cucumbers, and radishes. All beautiful, all edible, and all created by an eight-year-old and his grandfather. Nature gave us the canvas and means. We just had to create the garden and place the seeds. In those gardens, I found simple joy and inner peace. As a child, I didn't fully understand what growing food and creating gardens really meant to me. As an adult, I do, and I came to realize that a garden is a place where I find value and purpose in being. I appreciate the beauty and opportunity nature gives us. That experience continues to shape how I engage and interact with the earth.

Over the last twenty years, I fully embraced my passion for gardening and staying connected to nature. Every day I am digging new gardens, planting and tending old gardens, harvesting food, or volunteering at Freetown Farm. Four years ago, I moved to a property with two acres—most of it was lawn. I transformed much of that green canvas into large and small vegetable gardens, fruit trees, blackberry and raspberry canes, and blueberry bushes, and I began mixing edible plants into traditional ornamental planting beds. It's a never-ending, constantly evolving, and always rewarding journey that I get to share with fellow gardeners in my community, at Freetown Farm, and even across the globe through videos I make under The Rusted Garden Homestead.

Gary and Chiara are adding a new variety of blueberry bush, a fig tree, and a pawpaw tree to the fruit garden.

ABOUT THIS BOOK

We believe everyone can become an artist who connects with the land outside their door to create beautiful, abundant, edible landscapes. Your lawn and unused outdoor spaces are a blank canvas that can be transformed. Imagine vegetable gardens, herb gardens, fruit trees, berry brambles, edible flowers, and gathering spaces—a living ecosystem. *Growing an Edible Landscape* is about becoming that artist and looking at outdoor spaces through a new, creative, healthful lens. You can use this fresh perspective to transform a space into something that brings personal satisfaction and happiness and, of course, grows delicious food. Challenge the old idea that most residential outdoor spaces must be uniform, close-cut green grass punctuated by a few uninspired shrubs. And ask yourself this question: "Why did I choose grass lawns and non-edible plants?" The answer is, very often, "I didn't." They are just

put there when homes are built, and we inherit and maintain them by default because it is the norm.

No matter how small your outdoor space is, you can add something edible to it, even if you aren't the landowner. *Growing an Edible Landscape* provides the lens, inspiration, and tools you need to begin sculpting your space into something inspiring that you can share with family, friends, and neighbors. Gardens provide food and wellness of being. Food crops can leap outside the boundaries of a formal garden and be planted throughout a property in nontraditional places. Your journey begins by giving yourself permission to change the status quo, plant, and enjoy. This book will show you how to incorporate food production across your landscape. You don't need a formal vegetable garden. You can tuck some of your favorite vegetables just about anywhere there is room to plant.

1

THE CASE FOR LESS LAWN AND MORE FOOD

Step out of your home and look around. What do you see? If you are living in a westernized country and not in a densely urban or very dry environment, it is likely that your home is surrounded by a grass lawn. This presents both a problem and an opportunity. The problem is that lawns are an incredibly resource-intensive way to use land. They offer minimal benefits, other than sustaining old concepts of aesthetics and privilege. Rarely do people question why we have lawns. Do we need a uniform green blanket surrounding our homes? Do all the time and money we put into keeping the grass bright green and weed-free make sense? Do we understand the harm that comes with lawn care? The opportunity is that a lawn can be transformed—at least partially—into a food-producing area that is good for you, your community, and the environment!

Left: Cultivating edible plants instead of lawns helps with food self-sufficiency, reduces fossil fuel consumption, and builds communities.

A lawn, by definition, is simply an area of short grass, yet the impacts of mainstream lawn care are immense. Recent estimates for the United States alone are that 46 million acres (18 million hectares) of land are dedicated to residential, commercial, and public lawns, an area equivalent to the entire state of Washington. Although they produce no food or other commodity, lawns are now the largest irrigated crop in the United States, covering more area than corn and soybeans combined. Watering, mowing, weeding, and feeding the vast and still-growing swaths of land dedicated to lawns has significant negative environmental, economic, and health impacts. Reducing our lawns improves our shared well-being. In this chapter we explore the history and impacts of the lawn, as well as its alternatives. We feel this history is important as it shows how we were sold a dream of green grass that we didn't intentionally choose. Understanding this history offers a path to rethinking how we use the outdoor areas near our homes.

WHAT'S THE STORY WITH LAWNS?

The concept of a grass lawn originated in Western Europe, much of which has a moist, mild climate that is supportive of open, close-cut grasslands. The Middle English word *launde* originally referred to a glade or opening in the woods and became used to describe stretches of land that were created to resemble such glades. Some of the earliest lawns were the grasslands around medieval castles in France and England, kept clear of trees so inhabitants had an unobstructed view of approaching, potentially hostile, visitors. The term lawn also referred to the village commons, which was the meadow where villagers could graze their sheep and cattle. During the sixteenth-century renaissance, lawns began to be cultivated by the non-noble wealthy in both France and England, though they were more likely planted with edible plants such as chamomile or thyme than with grass. In seventeenth-century England, cropped grass lawns gained popularity at the homes of affluent landowners who increasingly depended on human labor to tend the grass around their homes, affirming the lawn as a mark of wealth and status.

The idea of the lawn, as well as the grass seeds to create it, traveled to North America and other parts of the world with immigrants from Europe. At first only the wealthy in North America had the time or money to cultivate a purely decorative lawn. Several factors, including sports, industrialization, and suburbanization, came together to make lawns common in the United States, a pattern and preference that has been replicated throughout many parts of the world.

In the United States, as cities grew and became increasingly industrialized in the mid-1800s, the lawn-centered park became a key part of city beautification campaigns. Around the same time,

Most untreated lawns already have edible and beneficial "weeds" in them, like this bright dandelion.

Lawns of grass replaced areas of edible plants and were a symbol of affluence and privilege.

Grass lawns have now become commonplace, but this space can become productive and be used to grow food.

the sports of lawn bowling and golf were imported from Scotland and England, increasing the demand for the lawns on which they were played. The development of lawn mowers in the mid-1800s made the proliferation of such public and sporting lawns possible. The migration of lawns from the civic center and sports fields into American backyards was driven by two overlapping developments in the middle of the 1900s. The first was the rise of the suburbs in the 1940s and 1950s, which were created to provide inexpensive housing to accommodate the families of soldiers returning from World War II.

The importance of a tidy, short lawn was promoted intensely in many of these subdivisions, along with advice on how to maintain this ideal. Lawns became so ingrained that communities created rules and regulations that dictated how a homeowner's space had to be maintained, down to the required height of the grass. A very rigid menu of what was allowed and not allowed in the areas surrounding homes became the norm—mostly grass and a selection of standardized shrubs, trees, and groundcovers, selected because they are ornamental and easy to maintain, not because they are a beneficial part of the environment.

Around this same time, war-based science and technology produced a series of new fertilizers and herbicides that made the idea of a uniform lawn, free from "weeds," possible. For example, until the early fifties in the United States, clover was an accepted and even encouraged part of lawns because it takes nitrogen from the air and deposits it in the earth where the grass can use it (reducing the need for manual fertilizing). Clover acquired its weed status because the earliest broadleaf herbicides killed it off along with the dandelions. Commercial lawn-care products became a big business as people were told to buy products to kill all weeds (anything other than blades of grass) if they wanted to have the best lawn, anything less being considered

shameful. Lawns became something we believed we had to have, something we had to spend money to maintain. The emphasis on lawn care and restrictive growing choices was, and often still is, rigorously enforced by homeowners' associations or the owners of housing developments or community spaces. This enforcement often completely prohibits our ability to grow food.

The grass-only lawn has now become a fixture of American culture—a symbol of the middle-class American dream that has been exported widely around the world, taking root in places where it makes even less sense than it does in the United States. For example, the lawn-care industry in Australia comes in second to that of the United States, followed closely

A suburb featuring uniform front and back lawns is ripe for growing food. Look at all that available growing space!

by Canada. Coming full circle to where lawns began, the lawn industry in the United Kingdom is about the fourth largest in the world per capita.

In other parts of the world, it remains the tradition for people to grow food in their yards. For example, in Russia, about half of the country's entire agricultural output is from home gardens, with one in three people relying on their own garden for food. This type of self-sufficiency is essential to humanity's evolution, with people having foraged for or grown their own food for the vast majority of our history, practices that are still commonplace throughout much of the world. We believe that in areas where lawns have become prolific, an edible landscape can become the new sought-after symbol, one that emphasizes well-being and creativity rather than an outdated idea of affluence.

A picket fence covered by berry brambles and surrounded by veggies and flowers at Gary's home is a testament to how beautiful an edible landscape can be.

IMPACTS OF CONVENTIONAL LAWNS

Grass in and of itself is not the problem. Even at large scales, grass can be a benign or even beneficial land cover. For example, the American Midwest was once a naturally wild prairie ecosystem filled with many types of wild grasses. The problem with grass lawns is the enormous amount of input required to maintain an always green, perfectly manicured monocrop. These inputs include gas-powered lawn equipment, water, fertilizers, herbicides, and pesticides. There are numerous interrelated impacts of conventional lawn maintenance practices. This section summarizes these impacts as they relate to natural resource use, environmental pollution, and health. We'll explain how reducing your lawn and creating a more natural and edible landscape does so much good in so many ways.

Natural Resource Consumption

Water: Only three percent of the Earth's water is fresh (rather than salt); however, most of that water is not accessible or usable because it is frozen in glaciers, is in the atmosphere or in the soil, or is too polluted. As the population increases around the world, the demand for fresh water is also increasing to meet our personal, agricultural, and industrial needs. In many places, we can directly see the impact of these demands, with wells and rivers running dry in our communities. Approximately 50 percent of residential water consumption in the United States is used for landscaping, most of it to water lawns, which equates to approximately 200 gallons (757 liters) of fresh, usually drinking-quality water per person per day. Given how precious water is to life and how constrained this resource is, it is concerning that so much fresh water is being used for such an unnecessary purpose.

Significant amounts of energy are required to maintain a low-cropped lawn. All of that changes when you convert to an edible landscape.

Fossil Fuels: Mainstream lawn care consumes oil and natural gas in numerous ways, including mowing, watering, fertilizing, and cleaning up. An average family in the United States with a one-third-acre (0.1 hectare) lawn will consume a total of 18 gallons (68 liters) of fuel per year maintaining their lawn, which includes the fuel for their lawnmower, the fuel needed to transport the water used on their lawns, the fuel used to make and transport fertilizer, and the fuel used for lawn clean-up activities such as leaf blowing and disposal of lawn waste. Some of the direct costs of using these fuels—such as the cost of labor to mine for coal or drill for oil, the cost of labor and materials to build energy-generating plants, and the cost of transportation of coal and oil to the plants—are included in the purchase price of gasoline and other energy sources. Other costs of using these fuels are more indirect and difficult to determine: for example, the health impacts of air pollution and the damage done to ecosystems and the environment as a whole by extracting and using fossil fuels. These costs are not reflected in the price of using finite fossil fuels.

This phenomenon can be explained, in part, by the fact that the average American household currently pays less than $2 a day for consistently available, unlimited, safe water, which does not come close to reflecting the true costs of having this resource. However, there are signs of change. For example, some cities in dry climates, such as Las Vegas, now pay residents to take out their lawns and replace them with rocks and native plants—ultimately this is much cheaper than figuring out how to get more access to fresh water.

Intensive water use, pesticides, and fossil fuels are required to maintain bright-green lawns, and for what benefit?

Air pollution from lawn-maintenance emissions is another factor to consider.

When infused with pesticide and fertilizer runoff, water sources face algae blooms and other negative impacts of contamination.

Environmental Pollution

Water Pollution: Water runoff polluted with fertilizers and pesticides is one of the single largest sources of water pollution, affecting groundwater, lakes and streams, wildlife, and human health. Of thirty commonly used lawn pesticides, seventeen are frequently detected in groundwater and twenty-three have the potential to leach into water sources, resulting in contaminated drinking water. For example, an estimated 60 percent of synthetic nitrogen applied to lawns ends up contaminating groundwater. As a whole, water pollution has substantial environmental, economic, and health impacts that should be actively minimized.

Soil Contamination: Using pesticides to create and sustain the classic green lawn actually causes harm to the soil life. Soil life is important to naturally aerate and fertilize the soil while also breaking down organic matter, thereby making it accessible to the grass. For example, chemical fertilizers can directly degrade soil by creating pH imbalances and a build-up of salts and nitrates, which can end up creating soil that is less fertile and more compacted. As a result, a vicious cycle is created in which more fertilizers are needed to keep grass green and more pesticides are needed to protect the weakened grass from pests and disease.

Air Pollution: A new gas-powered lawn mower produces as much air pollution in one hour of operation as eleven new cars being driven for one hour. Additionally, as fertilizers break down, they also release nitrous oxide into the atmosphere, a potent greenhouse gas that contributes to climate change. Similarly, as pesticides break down, they often release volatile organic compounds, a part of the "chemical soup" that creates ground-level ozone, which is part of the smog of air pollution you can often see over cities and industrial areas. As a whole, air pollution also has substantial environmental, economic, and health impacts that should be actively minimized.

Health Impacts

Ecosystem Health: In addition to the air, water, and soil contamination already discussed, lawn care has numerous harmful impacts on ecosystem health. Most lawns are made up of one or maybe two grass species, which reduces biodiversity, especially when the lawn covers a large area. Also, they are usually composed of introduced species that are not native to the area, which can further decrease an area's biodiversity and vital habitats supporting ecosystem health. Additionally, the pesticides and herbicides applied in abundance to most lawns kill not only the intended insects and plants, but also can be toxic to beneficial insects, amphibians, and plants. Of thirty commonly used yard pesticides, twenty-four are toxic to fish and other aquatic species, sixteen are toxic to birds, and eleven are deadly to bees and other pollinators. In recent years, pollinator populations have declined rapidly, which is inherently problematic as well as a critical concern for the growing of food.

Researchers believe that this phenomenon, called colony collapse disorder for bees, can be attributed to pesticides that are sickening or weakening bees and making it difficult for them to find and return to their hives. These bees are made weaker still because of the loss of biodiversity in farm fields and lawn yards, which is reducing their ability to get adequate nutrition.

Human Health: In addition to concerns resulting from air and water quality degradation, the primary impact to human health from mainstream lawn-care practices comes from pesticides. That pesticides are dangerous is well-established—their origins are in the weaponized nerve agents developed during World War II. Of the most commonly used lawn and garden pesticides and herbicides, fifteen cause neurotoxicity and nineteen are linked to an increased risk of cancer. Other health issues such as birth defects, neurological issues, increased

Dead bees and other wildlife are reflective of poor ecosystem health. Issues like colony collapse disorder and bird poisonings are often connected to pesticides.

asthma attacks, skin disorders, and disorders caused by endocrine system disruption, such as miscarriage and immune system problems, are also of real concern. The group most vulnerable to the health consequences of pesticide use is children. Their smaller body size and less developed immune systems make the impact of pesticide exposure more significant.

It is reasonable to believe that the average person who chooses mainstream lawn-care practices is not aware of the detrimental impacts of their choice. If people had to pay for the environmental cleanup and health-care costs associated with their choices, they would surely think more critically about their actions. It is our hope that this overview of the downsides to lawns will motivate you to make a conscious decision to transform lawns where you live, learn, work, or play into spaces that create numerous benefits rather than perpetuate harm.

No Mow May

No Mow May began in 2019 in the United Kingdom as a way to help bees and other pollinators, which are in sharp decline worldwide. By skipping lawn mowing for a month (during your early spring), you will likely find that many flowers such as dandelions, red clover, and violets have the chance to bloom (assuming your yard isn't heavily treated with herbicides). These flowers give pollinators an important boost early in the year, when not much is in bloom, which is critical for their well-being. Also, since 75 percent of the world's food crops depend on pollinators, it is critical for us to give them all the help we can. Not mowing for a month is an opportunity to learn a lot about your landscape, such as, what grows in your lawn besides grass; your personal preference for a longer, more diverse lawn; and that your lawn doesn't need as much water or fertilizer when it isn't cut short every week. If skipping mowing altogether is too much for you or neighbors, you can mow just the edges of your lawn so it looks more intentional, and then you can also have a direct comparison of the difference between the spaces.

Allowing part of your lawn to "go wild" is helpful for pollinators and other insects. No Mow May is a movement to avoid mowing your lawn for a month as an opportunity to learn more about your landscape.

An earthen bed garden with a mix of edible flowers and plants, including chard and beets, is a great alternative to turfgrass.

ALTERNATIVES TO THE LAWN

For those willing to partially or completely forgo the lawn, there are numerous attractive, enjoyable, and productive alternatives including patios and decks, pathways, mulched areas, groundcovers, natural meadows, flower gardens, trees and shrubs, rain gardens, xeriscaping, wildlife landscaping, food gardens, and much more. Depending on the area available, a mix of these landscapes is ideal to meet the needs of all inhabitants, human and otherwise. These landscape options have an array of books dedicated to them. This book focuses on using the land right around where we live, learn, work, and play for food production, an idea whose time has come once again.

This household built a raised bed filled with edible plants that also created a seating area. Enjoying and spending time in your edible landscape is so important.

For all of human history, up until about the last one hundred years, we have had to catch, gather, or grow most of our own food. Up until 11,000 BCE people acquired all of their food by hunting and gathering it from the wild. It was around this time that people in many areas of the world began to develop the knowledge and tools to grow crops and domesticate animals for food. By 5,000 BCE, agriculture was practiced on every inhabited continent other than Australia. While farming often required more work than hunting and gathering, it provided a tremendous increase in the amount of food calories people could obtain per acre of available land.

While farming mass quantities of key crops became important for feeding larger and denser populations, the kitchen garden remained commonplace for people in all but the densest cities well into the 1800s. Small, enclosed gardens right outside the door were the mainstay of a household's fresh goods, including produce and culinary and medicinal herbs. By the start of the 1900s, home gardens started to wane as produce became more readily available from stores, and kitchen gardens tended to move from just outside the front door to the side yard or backyard. Thinking back to the start of this chapter, this is around the same time that lawns became popularized and, indeed, lawns started to become the preferred (or required) front view for most homes.

However, it was during this same time that the World Wars led to a dramatic decline in food production due to agricultural laborers being recruited into military service. The idea of the victory garden was conceived as a way to increase the supply of food without the use of land and labor already engaged in agriculture, and without the significant use of transportation facilities needed for the war effort. In the United States, victory gardens were called for as a patriotic duty again during World War II, resulting in the planting of victory gardens by nearly twenty million Americans. These gardens produced up to 40 percent of all vegetables consumed nationally at the time. Victory gardens were planted in backyards, on apartment building rooftops, in vacant lots, and in public spaces.

Having almost completely disappeared since the end of World War II, in recent years new victory gardens have sprung up in public spaces. At the forefront of this effort are permaculture movements such as "Food Not Lawns," which was begun by Heather Flores. This movement to convert lawns to food offers the promise of improving the world by replacing lawns with fresh produce. Instead of the negative impacts of the lawn, a quarter acre (0.1 hectare) yard has the capacity in one year to yield 50 pounds (23 kilograms) of wheat, 60 pounds (27 kilograms) of fruit, 2,000 pounds (907 kilograms) of vegetables, and 75 pounds (34 kilograms) of nuts. These highly local food-production efforts have the multiple benefits of improving health, reducing carbon footprints, creating community, and saving money.

Historically, kitchen gardens were a prominent part of a household's land use. Stepping right outside your door to harvest was far more common than it is today.

This raised bed celebrates being a part of the victory garden movement.

THE BENEFITS OF GROWING YOUR OWN FOOD

If all this background about why it is a great idea to replace areas of lawn with edible landscapes isn't enough, here are some key personal benefits of growing your own food where you live, learn, work, and play.

It is great exercise! Whether you're preparing, planting, weeding, watering, or harvesting from your garden, you will be getting functional exercise that often utilizes your full body.

It's fun! There is a lot of joy and fun to be had in designing something beautiful and delicious, seeing it come to fruition, and connecting to the plants and animals in your community.

It's healthy! When we grow our own food, we tend to eat it soon after picking it, providing us with fresher, whole foods that have higher nutritional content than food that travels to us.

It's social! Growing and sharing food builds memories with family, friends, and the community. While it can be a solitary activity at times, it can also become a highlight for social interaction.

It saves money! After investing in gardening supplies, the ongoing costs of gardening are significantly lower than store-bought produce, especially if you save some of your seeds.

You are in control! It's a great feeling to know exactly how your food was grown. You are in charge of choices about fertilizer or pesticide use.

It offers security! Recent years have shown how sensitive mass food production and transportation can be to disruption and price increases, which makes having your own food a comfort.

It's good for your head! The mental health benefits of getting outdoors in the sunlight and dirt, and connecting with the earth and with yourself, are well documented and significant.

This yard space has been maximized with low garden beds filled with food crops.

The word "permaculture" was coined in the 1970s by Bill Mollison and David Holmgren, two Australian researchers that aggregated indigenous knowledge related to sustainable agriculture to create a system of ethical land use and design principles. The goal of permaculture design is to create agriculturally productive ecosystems that have the diversity, stability, and resilience of natural ecosystems. Many of the following ethics and principles can be incorporated into the design and care your edible landscape.

Permaculture is based on three core ethics:

- **Earth care**—Care for the earth and all living and nonliving things (animals, plants, water, air, and land).
- **People care**—Care for people and the promotion of self-reliance and community responsibility.
- **Fair share**—Ensure that all forms of surplus (money, crops, labor, information, etc.) are distributed to others instead of being wasted or hoarded.

To achieve these three ethics, twelve design principles have been defined. They include:

1. Observe and interact
2. Catch and store energy
3. Obtain a yield
4. Apply self-regulation and feedback
5. Use and value renewables
6. Produce no waste
7. Design from patterns to details
8. Integrate, don't segregate
9. Use small, slow solutions
10. Use and value diversity
11. Use edges and value the marginal
12. Creatively use and respond to change

Applied optimally, permaculture is intended to create the conditions for the harmonious integration of people into the natural landscape—providing their food, energy, shelter, and other material and non-material needs in a sustainable way.

Permaculture-based gardens often replicate more natural patterns, such as circles and spirals, as a way to fit in with the landscape and enhance the garden's unique beauty.

The fresh, colorful harvest that can come out of your edible landscape will save you money, give you more control over how your food is grown, and help build community.

History shows us how we were sold a dream of perfect green grass lawns. Now is the right time to start creating your own dream—growing your own food or thinking about new ways to integrate food into the outdoor areas you have access to. Even if it is not the primary growing season where you live, you can still begin preparing for your garden now. It's always a great time to determine where you want to grow food, how you want to build the spaces, what you want to grow and how you need to grow it, and what you need to make your food-growing dreams come true. Creating an edible landscape provides endless benefits, from improving health and well-being to saving money, increasing sustainability, and enhancing community. Let us help you start your journey in getting from here to there.

2

EXPLORING AND TRANSFORMING YOUR LANDSCAPE

Getting started with creating or expanding a garden can feel overwhelming. You don't have to transform your entire yard in a weekend, a month, or even within a year—it can be an ongoing project. The best way to begin is by selecting just one or two places on your property that seem like a good place to dig in. You can start in the corners of your yard, along the side of your house or a fence line, by expanding existing beds, or just by picking the sunniest spot. With time, a slow and steady pace will transform your lawn and unused outdoor spaces into beautiful edible landscapes.

Left: A sunny fence line filled with various edible plants at Gary's Rusted Garden homestead.

As you begin to create your vision for an edible landscape, you will find inspiration, come across new ideas, and imagine fresh possibilities. This is a creative process that only occurs by getting outside and making small changes. It is more important to get started and learn as you go than it is to learn everything there is to know about edible landscaping before you begin. The feeling that you need to know everything so you don't make mistakes is sometimes a barrier to starting the journey. Let's address that first by saying mistakes are just fine. The best way to begin is by stepping into your open space and thinking outside the box.

In addition to gathering knowledge, you will want to gather some basic gardening supplies before digging in.

Alternative Garden Locations

Even if you don't have access to any land, it is still possible to grow food! If you have a patio or balcony, there are containers that will work. If you live in an apartment complex, you may be able to get permission to grow a garden on the roof. If you have a neighbor with land, ask them if they would be open to you growing food on their property in exchange for a portion of the harvest. If this isn't possible where you live, consider looking at where you work, where you or your kids go to school, or places in your community that you frequent. You can also look into joining a community garden, but in many places there is a wait list, so explore that option sooner rather than later if it interests you.

Rooftops are a unique place to grow food, especially if you have limited ground-level space to cultivate.

The essential first step to creating an edible landscape is getting to know the place where you want to grow food. Whether this is a patio, your front, back, or side yard, or a place in your community, it is important to make sure you understand specific elements of your land. If the area is new to you, it is ideal to either observe it directly through a year of seasons or gather historical information from the internet or people who are more familiar with the place (neighbors, community garden members, etc.). If the area is familiar to you, you may think you know everything about it, but you will still want to make some specific observations that will inform your choices about creating your edible landscape.

The key things you want to understand are the big natural and human elements impacting your growing area: sun (and how it changes through the seasons); wind, rain, and water flows; plants and animals that call your area home; views you want to block or emphasize; and any significant risks such as pollution that you may need to manage. You will be able to come up with a more thoughtful, efficient, and productive edible landscape design when you take the time to consider these questions up front. You can make a garden journal or create a garden concept map to help track and update this information.

Sun

The majority of edible plants (but not all!) thrive in full-sun conditions. What might look like full sun in the spring may well be fully shaded once your trees and shrubs leaf out in the summer. The sunny part of your landscape that you enjoy when you are having your morning cup of tea or coffee may well be shaded by midday, meaning that it only fully supports plants that are happy with fewer hours of direct sunlight. One of the most basic ways to understand available sunlight and how it shifts throughout the day is knowing the directions of your growing area. Where is south, west, north, east? South- and west-facing areas tend to get the most direct sunlight (barring obstructions). If you know the daily and seasonal patterns of sunlight across your growing area, you can match your garden design elements and specific plant choices accordingly.

Wind and Water Flows

In some areas, prevailing winds will have a big impact on garden designs. If strong winds cut across your growing areas, consider creating windbreaks to reduce or redirect hot or cold winds that could negatively impact the plants you want to grow. If you have slopes on your property, that can impact how air flows too, but even more importantly it will impact how water flows. When growing food is your goal, water is tied with sunlight for importance, making it essential to understand how water flows through your garden area. Permaculture design emphasizes catching and storing water on a property, diverting excess water to prevent flooding or erosion issues, and creating thoughtful and water-wise irrigation systems. Any garden design should consider how much water plants will need and how much of that needs to be provided by you. If you have an area that naturally tends to hold water when it rains, this is a great place to put plants that are happier with a lot of moisture in the soil. If you have a particularly dry climate or parts of your land that dry out faster, you will want to think about plants and growing strategies that work well with these conditions to ensure the plants get the water they need. You don't want to design a garden where water-loving plants are placed in a dry area far away from your water source!

Creating a Sun Map

There are a lot of methods you can use to make a sun map of your growing area, for example:

- **Take pictures**—with a digital camera, tripod, and software or apps that allow for layering, you can pick a day (ideally in the spring, summer, and fall) to set up the camera with a clear view of your primary growing areas. Having some elevation, like a deck or upstairs windows, is helpful. On a sunny day, either program your camera to take a photo every hour or two, or set a reminder for yourself to do it manually, making note of the time each photo was taken. You can just look at the photos to inform your understanding of the sunlight, or you can use photo editing software to layer your photos, using an opacity feature to make them transparent enough to see the layers.

- **Make a sketch**—this is basically the same process as above, but instead of a camera, grab a pad of paper and a pencil and make a template of your growing area depicting fence lines, sheds, your home, etc. You can photocopy this to sketch the shade and sun patterns, or you can use tracing paper to add layers.

- **Get fancy**—you can calculate the shade using scientific tools and calculators, you can model the shade using online tools that track the sun's path by location and date, you can buy sun-tracking apps and services, and you can buy physical tools that allow you to directly measure sunlight exposure.

However you choose to make your sun map, look at your space at least every two hours starting at 8 a.m. and ending at 6 p.m.

Many edible "weeds," such as this purple dead nettle, are common finds in backyards. Just be sure the area has not been treated with pesticides or herbicides.

Violets are another favorite edible "weed" of ours.

Notice What Is Already Growing

One of the most interesting parts of exploring the land where you plan to create an edible landscape is learning which plants are already there, either naturally existing or purposely added. From trees to shrubs, flowers to lawn, figuring out what you already have growing will help you learn about what is well suited, or not, to the conditions in different parts of the property. Once you know what you have and whether it is healthy and useful to your own interests and goals, you can decide whether to keep the plants, find botanically related plants (see chapter 5) to add to the garden, or remove the plants to make more space for what you want to create.

If you have a lawn area that has not been treated with herbicides, you will likely find a wide variety of plants in the mix, many of which are edible. In the mid-Atlantic area of the United States where Chiara and Gary live, this includes clover, sorrel, dandelions, violets, plantain, chickweed, and purple dead nettle, just to name a few plants. In untreated or lightly managed property margins in this area, you are likely to find sweet cicely, bee balm, chicory, shiso, spicebush, stinging nettle, purslane, wild mustard, and lamb's quarters. The edges of woods are likely to include elderberry and autumn olive berry bushes and trees such as walnut and maple. All of these plants are edible!

By exploring and learning about what is already growing in your area, you have the chance to expand your relationship with plants beyond "good and bad" or weed, flower, vegetable. A weed can be thought of as a plant growing in a place where a person doesn't want it, or as Ralph Waldo Emerson put it about a weed, "A plant whose virtues have not yet been discovered." If you find a plant growing in your landscape that you don't know, see if you can identify it before you assume it is a weed that needs to be removed. Quite a few plants that "volunteer" themselves are native, or naturalized, and may be an important part of the local ecosystem. They might even be edible! Once you learn what plants are naturally abundant where you live and expand your plant knowledge to include some familiarity with "plant families" (chapter 5), you can start to connect the dots between what is already thriving without being tended and related plants that you could purposely plant in your garden.

Where Chiara lives, in every season she can take a walk around her property and those of a handful of neighbors and easily come home with a basket of foraged food, from dandelion, violets, lilacs, purple dead nettles, and onion grass in the spring, to peaches, mint, mimosa flowers, thyme, daylilies, clover, and plantain in the summer, to elderberries, roses, grapes, sage, wood sorrel, and lemon balm in the fall, and spruce and pine in the winter. By knowing her surrounding landscape (and her neighbors), the opportunities for what foods she can enjoy are tremendously expanded, well beyond what she has to actively manage growing.

The daylilies growing at Gary's Rusted Garden homestead are not only beautiful, they are also delicious.

Hostas are often planted in shady areas. Most people don't know that they are edible and can be eaten raw like other leafy greens or grilled or sautéed like asparagus.

Foraging is simply finding food in the "wild," which for practical purposes means any place where you have not intentionally planted it. This can mean harvesting truly wild foods that are found in forests or fields, picking berries growing on the edge of a nearby park, or gleaning the grapes spilling over your neighbor's back fence (one of Chiara's favorite childhood memories). Before you start picking or eating any foods you forage, it is very important that you learn the following foraging rules to ensure that you stay safe, act responsibly, and follow the law.

- *Be 100% certain that you have correctly identified a plant and 100% sure that it is edible.* This is the most essential rule because, while foraging opens up a fun and delicious world of edible plant possibilities, a wrong choice can make you very sick or can even be deadly. In addition to learning about what is edible, make sure you can positively identify the poisonous plants where you live. As you are learning, always reference at least two credible field guides to identify plants and how you can eat them (you can't eat all parts of all plants). If you aren't 100% sure of what a plant is or the safe way to enjoy it, leave it alone.

- *Be thoughtful about what you harvest, how much you take, and from where.* It is important only to pick from plants when they are abundant. **Never pick plants that are endangered or rare.** Take the time to know what these plants are in your community. You should only take what you can use and never take all of a plant from a particular place. It is essential that plants be able to reproduce and that wildlife that depend on them have access to their primary food source. Also, if you aren't on public land, you must have permission to enter a property, otherwise you are trespassing. Some public lands prohibit foraging, so be aware of the rules wherever you are, and ask for permission first.

- *Be careful with the plants you forage from and their surroundings.* Harvest using tools and techniques that ensure you aren't harming the plant. For example, do not remove all the leaves, fruits, or seeds from a plant and never pull a plant up by the roots (unless the roots are the edible part and the plants are almost invasive in their abundance). Be mindful not to trample or otherwise harm the plants surrounding the edible ones you are interested in and leave the habitat in good shape.

- *Be safe!* Do not harvest from areas that are likely to have contamination, such as along roads, lawns that are treated with chemicals, places where people walk their pets, conventional agricultural areas or industrial areas, etc. You should wash your foraged food before you eat it. Even if you are 100% sure that what you have picked is edible and you know the right way to enjoy it, try foods that are new to you in very small amounts at first. You are unique, and you may have an intolerance or reaction to a new plant even if most people are able to eat it (Gary loves daylilies, but they don't sit quite right with Chiara).

Chiara's neighborhood forage of (clockwise from top) mint, plantain, daylily, clover flowers, thyme, dandelion, peaches, and mimosa.

THREE CASE STUDIES OF
EDIBLE LANDSCAPE PROJECTS

To help you think more concretely about the potential for your own edible landscape, the following are three examples of lawn transformations.

Chiara's Yard: Small-Scale Shady

Chiara lives in a semi-urban townhouse community in a home that has a small and very shady front yard and a very narrow and fairly shady backyard. The front yard was patchy grass and scraggly shrubs when she moved in. Over time she has been transforming this space, starting with turning half of the front yard right up against the house into a patio using pavers. Chairs, a table, and a chiminea were added to make this an enjoyable outdoor gathering area, and about a dozen pots adorn the patio in various shapes and shades of blue. The pots are primarily planted with herbs that are happy enough in shadier conditions: mint, parsley, dill, oregano, thyme, and nasturtium. Window boxes were added several years into owning the property. The one right off the kitchen window is often planted with herbs, and the ones upstairs look lovely filled with sweet potato vine.

The other half of the front yard between the sidewalk and the patio has been planted over time with a mix of shade-loving edible plants such as ostrich ferns, additional herbs such as lemon balm, bee balm, sweet fennel, and sweet violet, and a selection of native plants like Solomon's seal, coral bells, and astilbe. In the four-foot (1.2-m) piece of land between her townhouse and that of her neighbor, they collaborated to put in a rain garden that catches the water coming off of both front roofs. The rain garden is filled with rocks and surrounded

Chiara's front yard is not a large space, but there are plenty of opportunities to incorporate edible plants.

This shady garden area features hostas and ostrich ferns, both of which are edible as young shoots in the spring.

Chiara's late-season neighborhood forage, including (clockwise from top) oregano, spruce, rose, concord grapes, basil, lemon balm, sage, elderberry, wood sorrel, and rosemary.

with plants that are happy to have wet roots, such as hostas, which are edible when their shoots emerge in the spring.

The backyard of the townhouse is just 16 feet (4.8 m) wide, and when Chiara and her family purchased the property it was unfenced and filled with grass, bare soil around trees, and a large area of English ivy, which is invasive where she lives. In collaboration with the neighbor, they fenced in the two yards together so there was enough space for kids to play and gardens to be grown. Along the new fence line, various bushes and plants were put in over time, with a focus on natives and edibles. Blueberry and lilac bushes were placed in the sunniest spots, spicebush in the shadier areas, and hardy kiwi was grown up the highest part of the fence. Once the English ivy was removed, sheet mulching

Native and Invasive

You may have heard the terms **native** and **invasive** in the context of plants or animals that live in your area. These terms are important to understand when creating your edible landscape. Native refers to a species that originated and evolved in the habitat where it is currently found and is therefore well adapted to the environment and an expected part of the local ecosystem. Invasive refers to a species that has been introduced to an area and is aggressive, outcompeting other species and causing harm to the balance of the ecosystem. It is important to note that there is a third category of species—those that are non-native but not invasive. These plants or animals have been introduced to an area but have integrated into the ecosystem in a way that is not harmful and sometimes can even be beneficial. In her book *Braiding Sweetgrass*, Robin Wall Kimmerer describes some of these plants as "naturalized," and she uses plantain, which is often found in untreated lawns, as an example of a beneficial naturalized plant in North America.

A native plant will generally thrive with less maintenance and will attract beneficial garden companions like butterflies and birds that rely on these plants as a source of food. Non-native plants tend to require more maintenance than natives because they are not adapted to where we are trying to grow them. Also, they don't offer as many benefits to the local environment. An invasive plant will take over an area and prevent other—native or non-native—plants from growing, which can disrupt both your garden plans and the ecosystem by replacing the native plants that native insects and animals depend on. Most common food-garden plants are neither native nor invasive, being additions that bring you tasty benefits but cause no harm to the surrounding environment.

was used to keep it from coming right back (see sidebar on this process). The mulched area was set up as a kids' play area, complete with a hammock between the two big, shade-casting trees and a mud kitchen. Native hydrangeas were planted around the perimeter of the play space to add beauty and a sense of a "secret garden" for the kids when they were younger. The space right along the back patios is the sunniest part of the backyards, so these were prepared with raised beds to grow some vegetables.

Cucumbers, cherry tomatoes, zucchini, and other squash are some of the most successful crops, and sun-loving herbs like basil were also added to this space. The central area of the combined yards was retained as a lawn for free play, but it is never treated with herbicides, pesticides, or fertilizers, and so it is a delightful combination of grass, dandelions, purple dead nettles, clovers, violets, and sorrel—everything other than grass being edible.

Ed's Yard: An Overgrown Hilltop

Ed has lived in his suburban home for decades, and now there isn't an inch of lawn to be found in his sloped front yard or backyard. His front yard is filled with ferns, hibiscus, and an abundance of other, mostly native, plants that are allowed fairly free range.

At the top of the hill that makes up most of Ed's backyard is a flat, sunny area that backs up to his neighbor's yard. This area hasn't been accessible to Ed for his gardening purposes, so it has become overgrown over time. When new neighbors moved into the adjacent house, they connected with Ed over a shared love of gardening. Their yard didn't have as much sunny space as they would have liked, so Ed offered about 400 square feet (37 square meters) of his land for them to use. Given the thick brambles, shrubs, and trees that filled this space, rented machinery was used to open it up for the garden. The bare, compact clay soil was then planted with a cover crop of rye to prevent erosion and improve the health of the soil. Reclaimed wood was used to build raised beds,

When he moved into his home decades ago, Ed's front yard was just a sloped grassy area. Now it is filled with edible plants such as ferns, roses, and hibiscus.

since it will take some time for the soil to be suitable for growing food. Cardboard, free firewood, and horse manure are being used to fill the beds. While construction is still in progress on this collaborative project, the transformation has already been substantial and is a lovely example of what is possible when community members connect and collaborate.

The back of Ed's yard during garden construction, showing the hill and future planting areas.

Heavy equipment was used to clear the area at the top of the hill and prepare it for the garden.

Once cleared, raised beds were built and filled with soil.

Soon enough, Ed's garden began producing a plethora of edible crops.

Sheet mulching is an inexpensive, natural way to prepare areas to become gardens. The basic idea is to use thick layers of natural materials (paper, cardboard, compost, etc.) to block sunlight from whatever plants you want to replace (grass, "weeds," etc.). These will die off in a way that nourishes the health of your soil and creates the foundation for the plants you want to grow. In warmer areas, the best time of year to sheet mulch is the fall, so everything can decompose over the winter, or the spring right before things start to green up. It takes about six months for areas you have sheet mulched to be optimal for new planting if you need to dig into the ground.

Once you have identified the area you want to sheet mulch (along a foundation or fence,

Sheet mulching at an elementary school garden installation by the Community Ecology Institute's Nourishing Gardens program.

at the base of raised beds, etc.), the items you will need for the project include:

- Lawn mower or weed wacker—to get plants down to a low level
- Tools—wheelbarrow, shovel, rake, spading fork or garden knife, etc.
- Biodegradable weed barrier—newspaper or cardboard
- Brown mulch—leaves, straw, wood chips

You can likely obtain both the weed barrier and the brown mulch at your local recycling center or by asking community members to share their landfill-bound resources with you. You might even be able to borrow the tools. Once you have all of your supplies handy, including a source of water, the following are the steps for sheet mulching:

1. **Get low:** Using your lawn mower or weed wacker (depending on what you are trying to get rid of), cut the existing plants down to the lowest level. You don't want them to grow back, so cutting them all the way down is helpful to your process. Leave any grass clippings as part of the natural mulch, but if you have plants like thistle that you want to get rid of, be careful to remove seed heads so they don't sprout right back. If you have woody plants that need to be removed from the area you are sheet mulching, pull them out by hand or dig them out with a shovel, trying to remove as much of the root base as possible. This is the time to get rocks or branches out of the area too so you have a smooth surface for the next step.

2. **Support the soil:** If the area you are working in has compacted soil, you can use a spading fork to gently loosen the soil and make holes for nutrients to enter. You shouldn't till or turn over your soil because it disrupts the soil ecosystem, which you are working to enhance with sheet mulching. If you are planning to put bigger plants into your new garden area (fruiting shrubs or trees), you can put

them in at this time and then mulch around them so you aren't digging through all the layers of the sheet mulch later.

3. **Layer away:** The biggest part of the project is to create the layers of organic matter—the sheets, or the lasagna layers if it helps to think about it that way:

a. Evenly spread about 1 inch (2.5 cm) of compost, leaves, or straw on the ground. This will attract worms and beneficial insects to help loosen up the soil. Spray the whole area with water to help kick-start the process of decomposition and help the next layer stick.

b. Lay out thick layers of newspaper or cardboard (at least ¾ inch [2 cm] thick) over the entire area to create a weed barrier. It is really important to substantially overlap the edges of your paper product so there are no gaps that allow sunlight to get through and encourage your old ground-cover to grow back. Also make sure that you have removed glossy pages from the newspaper and tape from cardboard (don't use glossy or wax-covered cardboard at all), since these elements don't decompose well. Spray the whole area with water again.

c. Evenly cover the weed barrier layer with 2 to 3 inches (5 to 7.5 cm) of compost, which will help the decomposition process and support soil health.

d. Add an even layer of 3 to 4 inches (7.5 to 10 cm) of organic material such as leaves or wood chips. This layer helps ensure that light doesn't penetrate to the ground, and it supports beneficial microorganisms. At this point your mulch layer should be about 8 inches (20 cm) tall. Water it one more time and wait!

If it is important to add some visual appeal to the area while the sheet mulching is doing its work, you can add a couple of inches of compost to the top and add small plants into the space, using a gardening knife to cut small holes in the paper layer so the roots have a way to access the soil.

In this example of sheet mulching over a larger area, the cardboard is covered with a thick layer of straw.

Kim's Yard: A Sunny Suburban Home

Kim and her husband bought their home in the summer of 2016. The 0.38-acre (0.15 ha) property was mostly a blank slate, except for a row of boxwood shrubs along the foundation and a small circle of black-eyed Susans surrounding a lamp post. They felt both excited and daunted when they imagined how they might transform this little bit of earth into something beautiful. It was around this same time that Kim started to learn about native plants and was introduced to the concept of edible landscapes. Suddenly her blank slate had a purpose: to become a suburban oasis that was beautiful, bountiful, and ecologically balanced. She started to imagine their yard as a sanctuary for pollinators and turtles, snakes and squirrels. Over the next three years she added more and more native plants. As she did, the creatures that she hoped to attract began to show up: bumble bees, hover flies, moths, butterflies, toads, frogs, snakes, skinks, squirrels, snails, field mice, hummingbirds, hawks, and more. Their property had come to life! Kim's vision grew. She started to think about their 4' x 8' (1.2 x 2.4 m) vegetable garden, wondering how they could improve and expand it using the same ecological principles that informed her landscape design.

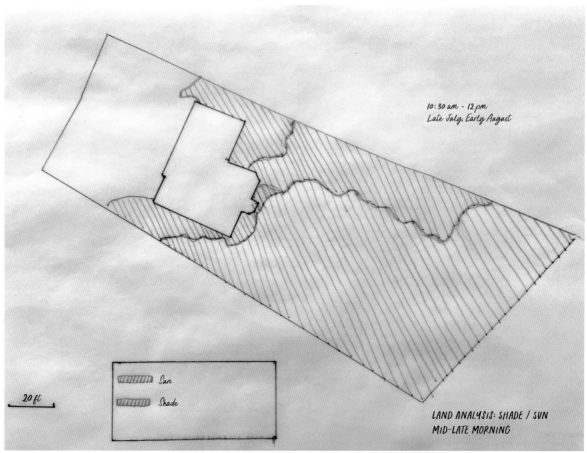

10:30 am - 12 pm
Late July, Early August

20 ft

| | Sun |
| | Shade |

LAND ANALYSIS: SHADE / SUN
MID-LATE MORNING

This hand-drawn map of the sun/shade pattern across Kim's property is helpful for choosing the best location for plantings. The design was rendered for a permaculture design certification.

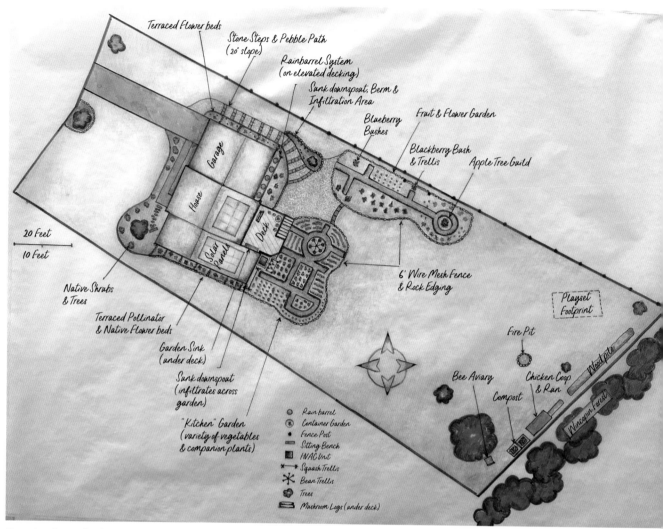

The following labels appear on the hand-drawn design:

Terraced Flower beds
Stone Steps & Pebble Path (20' slope)
Rainbarrel System (on elevated decking)
Sunk downspout, Berm & Infiltration Area
Blueberry Bushes
Fruit & Flower Garden
Blackberry Bush & Trellis
Apple Tree Guild
Garage
House
Solar Panels
Deck
20 Feet
10 Feet
Native Shrubs & Trees
Terraced Pollinator & Native Flower beds
Garden Sink (under deck)
Sunk downspout (infiltrates across garden)
"Kitchen" Garden (variety of vegetables & companion plants)
6' Wire Mesh Fence & Rock Edging
Playset Footprint
Fire Pit
Bee Aviary
Chicken Coop & Run
Woodpile
Compost
Wincopin Forest

Legend:
- Rain barrel
- Container Garden
- Fence Post
- Sitting Bench
- HVAC Unit
- Squash Trellis
- Bean Trellis
- Trees
- Mushroom Logs (under deck)

Next, the plan evolved into this hand-drawn final design concept that shows all of the planting areas around the property.

The onset of the pandemic forced a step back in Kim's career in early 2020, but it presented an opportunity to explore her curiosity further. She enrolled in an online permaculture design certification program and spent hours each day absorbing content, taking notes, and staring out her back window envisaging these concepts applied. By the fall of 2020 she had gotten to work. Using a sheet-mulching technique, she began the process of transforming two large areas of their backyard from dense clay lawn into supple earth, rich with organic matter. She mapped sun patterns and watched how water moved through the property during heavy rains. She began drafting plans to create a productive landscape, complete with a composting system, perennial fruit garden, multi-season vegetable garden, water harvesting features, chicken raising, beekeeping amenities, and pollinator gardens. She learned about hardscaping and stone work and transformed an eroded hillside into a beautiful stone walkway with steps to connect the gardens to her home, prevent soil loss, and improve water permeation.

This is Kim's "blank slate" backyard, looking toward the fence line, before the project began.

First, the kitchen garden was outlined with rocks.

By early spring 2021 she had much of her vision in place. The garden was designed to be both beautiful and functional—a destination to commune with nature, not simply a place of utility. She knew that growing food in a newly sheet-mulched garden would prove challenging; the soil would take years to be fully formed. But she wrote her seed list with ambition, determined to simply get her hands in the soil and learn.

Through the spring and summer of 2021, she grew twenty-eight different plants spanning fruit, flowers, vegetables, and herbs. To her delight much of the garden was a success, and she enjoyed a plentiful yield while also learning what would need to change going forward. The year 2022 proved to be another year of learning and growth; Kim and her husband reformatted the layout of some of the beds, added a small wildlife pond and sitting space in a shady corner, and learned that managing a productive landscape while eight months pregnant required a lot of letting go and giving in to plants in their most wild and unwieldy forms. And yet, the bees still came, the flowers still grew, and the food still made it to the table in abundance.

Creating our own edible landscapes starts with the understanding that our growing areas vary, our skill sets vary, our budgets vary, our climates vary, and our tastes in style and food vary. Chapter 3 provides basic design principles for building your growing spaces. Chapter 4 will help you understand the needs of your gardens, and chapter 7 will provide skills needed to grow and maintain your edible landscapes. These chapters will help you get started with digging and planting. Remember, the best way to learn is by doing!

Next, the fruit garden was outlined. Organic horse manure was spread as the first layer of the sheet mulching process.

Adding the next layer (cardboard) to the sheet mulch process. Note the larger blueberry bushes in the bed.

Here, the kitchen garden sheet mulching is underway and nearing completion of the layers.

Both garden beds are now complete with layers of sheet mulch—a layer of organic horse manure, a layer of cardboard, another layer of horse manure mixed with soil, a layer of straw, and finally a layer of fallen leaves (added the following month when the leaves dropped).

The beds for the kitchen garden utilized locally harvested rock from the yard and wood line as an outline. A layer of topsoil was added to help boost growing performance for year one.

The kitchen garden design is now complete and the protective fence installed. Kim and her family did all the labor themselves, including the design and installation of the fence.

The now-complete fruit garden design, including a newly planted Jonathan apple and a trellis for blackberries.

The first year, the kitchen garden consisted mostly of vegetables and herbs.

The first year, the fruit garden contained mostly perennial and annual fruits, including blueberry, blackberry, apple, and watermelon.

Friends hanging out in Kim's garden, enjoying the afternoon sun and keeping the frogs company. Five frogs called this little wildlife pond home the very first year.

3

GARDEN DESIGNS FOR EDIBLE YARDS

Generally speaking, people who want to grow food will plant fruits and berries, vegetables, leafy greens, and herbs in a single garden. But these food crops can also be scattered across an entire property if desired, or they can be planted in themed areas on your ground. Berries might be in an area where you enjoy taking a morning walk, and you can pick and eat them as part of an informal foraged breakfast as you wander. Leafy greens may be in an area selected for ease of picking to make salads for dinners. Herbs are wonderful to scatter around, but a centralized patch of cooking herbs close to the house makes good sense. Mingling edible plants and flowers within decorative planting beds does not have to be a formal process.

Left: Herbs and edible flowers, now ready for harvest, dot Gary's landscape.

Look at your outdoor space as rooms. It's a way to help organize what you grow, where you grow, and how you get to the plants for harvesting. Take note of what plants grow well and what you really enjoy eating, and put them on your "must plant" yearly list. Replace plants that struggle every year, or move them to different locations to see if they fare better. Your edible landscape will change and improve every year, and that is part of the creative adventure!

Your design may include a spot for a traditional vegetable garden, or you can plant traditional garden vegetables in pockets of open space across your property. There is no doubt our favorite vegetables are garden mainstays, but also consider growing food plants that are new to you. For example, edible amaranth comes in so many different colors, sizes, and blooms, it's a beautiful enhancement to any garden. It's the addition of these nontraditional edible plants that will truly transform your yard. Chapter 5 provides nontraditional food crops and chapter 6 has themed planting menus to help you get started.

We recommend starting small and tapping into your creativity. A small, more traditional garden that provides some of your favorite herbs, fruits, and vegetables is only one piece of an edible landscape. It is the standard way many people grow plants for food and culinary uses, but these gardens are not always welcomed. Some properties have home-owners' associations that inhibit our freedom to plant and tend our open spaces for food production.

Chard mingles with flowers along a white picket fence.

There are many ways to work around restrictions when food gardens are designed. You may have to "hide" a bunch of edible plants in plain sight with an edible flower garden right in your front yard. You can incorporate local restrictive rules into your overall design or even challenge them locally. This is where breaking from traditional growing beds can have great benefit. For example, pepper plants and rainbow chard can be tucked into any space with eight or more hours of sun, and they look ornamental. Spinach can look like a groundcover. Amaranth, with its edible leaves for salads or sautéing, can replace the common ornamental plant coleus. Strawberry plants can replace most groundcovers. Weaving grapevines and tomatoes along a picket fence can replace climbing ivies and flowering vines. Many food-bearing plants can be planted in this way.

Your new spaces can be designed as centerpieces in the landscape or tucked away somewhere hidden from the spotlight. You may choose to use containers or design large swaths of earth beds that cut across your yard. This chapter provides ideas, designs, and principles to help you start transforming your land-scape. Let's begin with an easy way to get started using containers and then address many of the common foundation plantings that already exist in many places. And remember, these designs are meant to be adapted and blended into your own vision of an edible landscape. There is no need to fear a mistake—plants can be moved, and beds can be redesigned.

Amaranth is not only pretty, it's edible. You'll find a profile for this attractive crop in chapter 5.

Containers filled with herbs and edible flowers work beautifully along a fence or house and are easy to change or move when necessary.

CONTAINER GARDENING

Container gardening is a great way to get your hands dirty and learn about growing plants. It is a great option if you are renting property as they can be emptied and easily transported to a new location. Whether you are growing on a balcony, a patio, or a large amount of land, containers have their place. Containers can be used on a small scale or a large scale. They can be arranged together as a focal point in a single growing area or used throughout the entire landscape, tucked into any space you want to enhance.

The container itself becomes part of the beauty of the garden. Some people enjoy the look of half whiskey barrels, aged and rusted metal tubs, classic moss-covered terracotta pots, or brightly colored plastic containers. The options are almost endless.

The keys to successful container gardening are a loose container mix that holds moisture, consistent watering, regular fertilizing, and several drainage holes. All containers need to have several drainage holes in case one becomes blocked. Roots need oxygen as do most beneficial soil microbes.

Gary's container garden features a fig tree in a whiskey barrel.

Herbs are an integral part of an edible garden.
Gary's collection features prominently in his landscape.

This mix of containers and raised beds maximizes a sunny corner of a property right next to the house.

Small-scale container gardens easily fit on patios, decks, and porches if you grow in tight quarters.

Without adequate drainage, standing water fills the pockets of air in the soil and the water stagnates in the container, which causes roots to rot and the soil life to die. Chapter 7 will address soil amendments and basic care of your gardens. If you plan on using a bagged soil product, purchase a bag that is labeled as either a container mix or potting mix. Buy whatever fits your budget—they are both equally effective and pretty much have the same ingredients.

Watering and fertilizing container-grown plants will vary greatly based on the plant size and container size. Be prepared to water container gardens two to three times a week when temperatures are cooler and almost daily during the high heat of summer when plants are mature. Container plants have limited soil for root growth, and they quickly use up nutrients in the soil as they grow. The plants should be fed with a water-soluble organic fertilizer every 7 to 14 days with the frequency moving toward every 7 days as the plants begin to reach maturity.

Budget Saver #1: Use Container Gardens as a Plant Nursery

We are aware of the costs associated with creating an edible landscape and will offer solutions to help mitigate the costs of getting started throughout the book.

Tip One: A lavender plant in a gallon (4-L) pot can cost three or four times more than a lavender plant in a pint (0.5-L) container. This holds true for many plants, bushes, and trees. The less expensive smaller plants can be potted up and grown in your container gardens until they mature to a size that merits transplanting into other parts of your garden.

Tip Two: Plants are often put on sale at the end of the growing season. These are perfect times to find inexpensive plants and get them into containers. While these plants could be planted throughout your garden, centralizing

them as part of a container garden makes care much easier while they are growing to a larger size. It is also a good method for holding plants until future beds are built. Shop sales, hold plants, and save money.

Tip Three: Another way to use containers as a plant nursery is to nurture damaged plants back to health. Most garden centers have damaged plants that are discounted or even thrown out. Often they just need to be fertilized and watered regularly. You can pot up damaged plants and care for them until they perk back up. When you are out buying plants, ask employees what they do with damaged plants. You may not always find edible crops, but you will be surprised at the number of edible flowers you can find.

The beauty of growing in containers is that they come in so many styles, shapes, sizes, and materials. Fabric pots are wonderful as they are inexpensive and light. Blending 5-gallon (19-L), 10-gallon (38-L), 20-gallon (76-L), and even 100-gallon (379-L) fabric pots together can be the starting point for building your edible landscape. You can grow just about anything in containers, from dwarf fruit trees, blueberry bushes, vegetables, and herbs, all the way down to root crops like potatoes and sweet potatoes, as well as some delicious mushrooms.

Containers of lettuce are easily tucked throughout a property and can provide months of salad greens.

Formal shrub plantings like this one are common sights, but thankfully, there is so much opportunity for incorporating edible plants into the mix.

FOUNDATION PLANTING

A great place to start building your edible landscape is in the garden beds that likely already exist on your property along your house or fence. Traditional foundation beds or landscape beds around homes

This mainstream foundation planting lacks ecological or edible benefits—not to mention interest.

are often filled with "cookie cutter" non-edible plants. Keep the trees, bushes, and flowers you truly enjoy. Remove the old plants, especially any that are invasive, expand the beds slightly, if needed, and free up new space for your edible crops. This is a very quick way to get digging, planting, and sculpting. If you want to expand or create foundation beds, get them started with the sheet mulching technique described in chapter 2.

Foundation beds have their own unique characteristics, which should be incorporated into the overall design of your edible landscape. Here in the Northern Hemisphere, the north side of a house is almost full shade and the soil temperature stays cooler. Growing edible food on this side of a house requires finding plants that love the shade. Fortunately, ferns meet this requirement. Not all ferns are edible. The bracken, ostrich, and lady fern

Incorporate ostrich ferns into foundation plantings on the shady side of your home for a spring treat of edible fiddleheads.

varieties are some of the more popular edible ferns. Mature fern leaves are not edible. The emerging fiddleheads or fern fronds are harvested from the fern over a 1- to 2-week period. We recommend growing the ostrich fern as your first edible fiddlehead, as it is widely eaten. Many fern fronds are toxic, need special preparation, or should be eaten in limited quantities. The ostrich fern is eaten with regularity, should be sautéed, and has a reputation of tasting like a mix of asparagus, broccoli, and green beans.

The east side of a house may get 4 to 6 hours of sunlight. This side tends to stay cooler and plants are protected from the more intense afternoon sun. Certain leafy greens can be grown on the east side of a home. In fact, leafy greens can thrive there well into summer, when most other leafy greens planted in full-sun areas bolt and flower from rising temperatures. Matching the needs of plants to what a planting area offers is another key in the design of your edible landscape.

Budget Saver #2: A Simple Refresh of Existing Beds

A simple refresh of existing beds can get you growing with little cost.

Step One: Remove weeds and compost them. If mulch is present, rake it to the side of the bed—it will be reused.

Step Two: Sink a shovel 8 to 10 inches (20 to 25 cm) deep and gently lift the soil a bit but don't turn it. This gentle lift is to aerate it. Do this every 6 inches (15 cm) until the entire bed is aerated.

Step Three: Purchase any organic fertilizer that is on sale and cover the growing area. Follow the instructions on the label for application.

This can be a granular or water-soluble fertilizer. Fertilizers are discussed in more detail in chapter 7.

Step Four: Edge the beds to a depth of 6 inches (15 cm) and scatter the removed earth across the bed. Spread any mulch that was raked to the side across the surface and rake the bed even. An additional 2 inches (5 cm) of new mulch should be added. This can be cut grass, chopped leaves, or any shredded mulch product that is on sale.

We will discuss additional amendments that can be added throughout the book, but this is a simple budget-friendly refresh that will allow you to get planting.

Though it looks like a standard perennial garden, this garden bed hosts a colorful variety of plants, including some that are edible, such as monarda, parsley, and elderberry.

Various sun-loving vegetables have been incorporated into this border planting.

This house in Ithaca, New York, has beautiful front plantings.

The southern and western sides of a home can support just about any plant that loves the sun. The southern side is interesting because it gets the most sun and the soil gets very warm. Certain plants may not enjoy that amount of heat during the summer and may be best planted off the western foundation. Both of these foundation beds can support vegetables, fruits, flowers, herbs, berry bushes, fruit canes, and fruit trees. During the winter, the south side of a house has a unique benefit. The southern foundation of the house often absorbs heat during the winter day and radiates it back during the freezing night. Homes that have brick, cinderblock, concrete, or stone foundations are the best for this. If you are growing plants that are on the border of dying off from the temperature lows of your winters, plant them along the southern foundation of your house, close to the house. The microclimate created in that growing bed may be enough to protect the plants and bushes from your winter.

Many plants like lavender, rosemary, and fig trees can take freezing temperatures, but prolonged deep freezes can kill or significantly weaken them in colder climates. They are perfect candidates for southern foundation planting.

EARTH BEDS

It is important to think about the scale of your design and the number of earth beds and other growing beds you want to create. Don't put pressure on yourself to quickly complete them all at once. We recommend breaking your vision into stages and building the pieces of your edible landscape more slowly when first starting. The initial acts of successfully digging, planting, and sculpting your vision in the earth will bring you joy, satisfaction, and the ongoing encouragement needed to maintain motivation. Early success will help maintain the momentum needed to complete your plan. Our visions of our properties and Freetown Farm were slowly built year after year and still aren't fully completed.

This white bench in front of an earth bed in autumn is the perfect place to rest and contemplate garden plans.

In summer, the same bench offers a place to sit, surrounded by the fruits of your labor, including fruit trees, dill, and other edible plants.

The earthen mounds and raised beds in this new garden create a "grow it, eat it" garden framework.

The same garden is now being planted with a mixture of edible plants.

Overdoing the number and size of earth beds is common when starting. Remember that these beds have to be planted and maintained over the season, and they can be expensive. An important design principle is to create what you can take care of without it becoming a burden or an unpleasant chore. Another important design principle is to have a budget that covers the creation, planting, and tending of each bed added into the edible landscape. One of the easiest and most inexpensive ways to create food-growing areas is to make new earth beds in an open lawn or unused space found on your property.

An earth bed is nothing more than a detached foundation bed. They can be built to your needs and placed throughout any part of a property. The bed shapes are endless for this type of growing space. Use sand, flour, hose, rope, or anything that will allow you to create a rough outline of the bed. Step back and observe the shape from different parts of your yard. Think about how it will look when mature and how it will impact the space. It is much easier to expand a bed than it is to shrink it.

There are many ways to construct and fill the beds, but they all start with edging out the shape. Dig a 6- to 8-inch (15- to 20-cm) trench around the outline of the bed. Compost the edged material or use it in the construction of the bed. The trench defines the space, collects rain, and creates a barrier to unwanted encroaching roots. Now that the beds are shaped, transforming them into growing beds can be done dozens of different ways. Here are some options that you can use and modify to meet your needs.

We cannot stress the number of ways to build beds and grow plants enough. What is important is that, whatever you choose, recognize that the soil does not have to be perfect to start. Each year the soil quality of the beds will improve as organic matter is regularly added and as you make more compost for use in your edible landscape. Compost is the best amendment to use in any of your designs. An effective alternative to compost is decayed leaves, commonly called leaf mold. They nourish soil life, improve the soil, and feed the plants. Compost, however, has more nitrogen, phosphorus, and potassium.

Right: An earth bed Gary created using cardboard and homemade compost is a perfect planting site for edible crops.

BASIC METHODS FOR BUILDING EARTH BEDS

Option One: **Quick Planting and Budget Friendly**	This is the least expensive way to create earth beds and immediately get to planting. Remove the grass and weeds from the bed, leaving only your native earth. The removed materials should be composted. This method is best used for dropping transplants, bushes, and trees into planting holes. The earth is still compacted and is only turned, loosened, and amended where the plants are being placed. If you want to plant seeds, select the area for seeding, turn and loosen the soil to at least a depth of 6 inches (15 cm). Mulch all non-seeded areas with 1 to 2 inches (2.5 to 5 cm) of cut grass or shredded leaves. Water in each transplant and seeded area well with an organic water-soluble fertilizer, one time, to start. Water the bed evenly several times a week for the first month.
Option Two: **Limited Labor and Budget Friendly**	If you can wait 8 to 12 weeks, use a modified method of sheet mulching using more cardboard layers. It is best used for transplants and not direct seeding. Cardboard can break down in as little as 4 weeks based on temperatures. You can use this method to reduce your workload when building ahead of planting. The grass does not need to be removed or cut. Layer 4 to 5 layers of cardboard across the bed, soaking each layer thoroughly as placed. Be sure to overlap the gaps between sheets as you add layers. The additional layers of cardboard will kill off any undergrowth, and it will decay quickly if kept moist. Spread a layer of 1 to 2 inches (2.5 to 5 cm) of any yard soil or inexpensive bagged topsoil evenly across the cardboard. Add the same amount and type of mulch as in option one. You can use bagged mulch if nothing else is available, but it should be a well-shredded wood variety versus a large type of wood chip.
Option 3: **A Quick and Premium Seeding Bed**	Eliminate the grass and weeds by hand or by any method of sheet mulching you prefer based on how quickly you want to get planting. A single layer of overlapping cardboard is effective using this option because of the volume of material being placed into the bed. Add 6 to 8 inches (15 to 20 cm) of quality compost, garden soil, or a combination of both across the bed. The bed should be raked into a mound formation. Soak the entire bed down thoroughly 24 to 48 hours before planting seeds. Mulch should not be used when planting seeds. If you choose to plant transplants in this design, mulch can be added as directed in option one above. This option is more expensive but quickly creates a premium planting area.

* More information about making soil mix, using amendments, and fertilizing is discussed in chapter 7 and can be applied here based on what is being grown.

HÜGELKULTUR

An interesting variation of earth beds is hügelkultur. This method, while initially labor intensive, pays dividends in water management and fertilization for years to come. In short, hügelkultur is creating a growing bed by mounding and burying organic matter in soil. The organic matter is often large logs, small branches, leaves, and fresh-cut grass. In chapter 4, rainfall and watering are discussed. This type of bed works well where rainfall is scarce and the ability to water is limited. The abundance of buried, different-sized organic matter holds water well. Over time the decaying logs hold moisture like sponges. The decomposing organic matter not only holds water well, it also feeds the plants over the years. It is a wonderful way to use your local resources to create self-sustaining garden beds.

There are three styles of hügelkultur bed:

- **Traditional**—the mound is built directly on the ground. This is the easiest way to create this type of garden bed but does the least in terms of water retention.
- **Sunken**—in this approach you dig a trench that you fill to the top with your woody debris and soil so that the garden is directly level with the ground. This approach has the best water-retention benefits, so it is great for drier areas.
- **Hybrid**—this is a mix of the first two styles. You dig into the ground a bit for your bulkier wood elements, and the top of the garden bed is slightly mounded, similar to your typical earthen garden. This approach is the sweet spot in terms of level of work and level of water retention.

Regardless of what style of hügelkultur bed you want, there are basic steps to building this kind of bed.

- Choose an area that has the right amount of light for what you want to grow.
- Mark where you want each bed—they should be no more than 3 feet (1 m) wide. The beds can be as long as you want, but having spaces every 6 feet (2 m) or so makes maintenance and harvesting easier.
- Collect the materials you need for the project:
  - Logs, branches, twigs, and fallen leaves from your yard are perfect—it puts them to use instead of being trashed or burned. Do not use walnut, cedar, or other tree species that make soils toxic to other plants.
  - Gather nitrogen-rich material such as kitchen compost or manure.
  - Collect enough topsoil to cover your bed with about 2 inches (5 cm).
  - Mulching material such as straw or wood chips will be needed as well.
- Lay your biggest pieces of wood down as the first layer—this should be logs or branches. Then add your smaller branches, sticks, etc. A great depth for the wood pile part of the garden (whether in the ground, above the ground, or half and half) is about 3 feet (1 m).

Lay out the woody layer of a hügelkultur bed first.

Adding wood chips to a hügelkultur mound.

- Water the wood layers well. This will expose gaps that you then fill with the leaves and nitrogen elements like manure and kitchen-scrap compost.
- Top the bed with about 2 inches (5 cm) of topsoil and a layer of mulch material.

Ideally you should wait a few months before planting your hügelkultur so the bed can settle and the internal composting can get going. If you create a hügelkultur bed in the fall or winter, it will be perfect for spring planting, but if that timing and delay doesn't work for you, it is OK to plant right away just like you would any other bed in your garden.

This finished hügelkultur mound will be ready for planting within a few months.

A tall raised bed in Gary's garden is home to sixteen pepper plants.

RAISED BEDS

Raised beds can provide a more formal definition to edible landscape designs, though the visual impact of the beds can vary greatly based on the materials and shapes you choose. Raised beds and containers are often used together. In Gary's garden, the structures he uses for growing—containers, framed bed, earth mounds, trellises, posts, and fencing—are used as points of interest throughout the landscape. When winter comes to his gardens, he enjoys the almost poetic look of these structures covered in the freshly fallen snow, dried brown vines, and remains of the once-flourishing garden. It is an inspiration for him to reflect on what was and what is to come, mulling over endless ideas for expanding his edible landscape come spring.

High-sided raised beds are typically made from wood or corrugated metal. Raised beds can vary in height and can be generally placed into two categories: high sided and low sided. To get the full benefits of a raised-bed garden, the sides should be high—12 inches (30 cm) tall or taller. One of Gary's favorite beds to grow peppers in is a 36-inch (1-m) tall dark gray metal raised bed.

Raised beds can add interest to unused spaces in the corners of yards or create focal points in traditional non-food-bearing beds. Low-sided raised beds also have benefits. Most raised beds sit on the earth with open bottoms. A third type is a raised bed that sits on legs. They are usually 3 to 4 feet (1 to 1.25 m) tall, raising a planting bed upward for the gardener to more easily grow food in the space. However, the actual planting area may only have a 12- to 16-inch (30- to 40-cm) soil depth for planting.

Right: Gary's snow-covered main vegetable garden brings him both joy and flavorful pickings.

BENEFITS OF RAISED BEDS IN AN EDIBLE LANDSCAPE

Plant	Low Sided Under 12 in (30 cm)	High Sided 12 in (30 cm) or Taller
Conserves Resources & Saves Money	✓	✓
Improves Soil for Healthier Plants	✓	✓
Organizes Growing Space	✓	✓
Increases Food Production Potential	✓	✓
Improves Soil Drainage	✓	✓
Decreases Soil Compaction	✓	✓
Grow More on Poor-Quality Soil	✓	✓
Aesthetically Pleasing	✓	✓
Lengthens Growing Season	✓	✓
Better Protection from Animals		✓
Physically Easier to Tend		✓
Grow on Very Poor-Quality Soil		✓
*Grow Food Anywhere		✓

*Raised beds placed on legs or raised beds with 24-in (60-cm) sides can be placed anywhere to grow food.
 Using raised beds, part of your edible landscape can be a patio, driveway, or rock-laden yard.

Low metal raised beds can be used anywhere across an edible landscape. They offer a quick and simple option to get planting ASAP.

Raised beds can be as long as you wish, but they should not be more than 4 feet (1.25 m) wide. In order to tend raised beds, you should be able to reach all the plants without having to walk on the soil surface. One of the benefits is the reduction of foot traffic, which reduces compaction, keeping the bed better aerated for root development. The average adult arm reach is about 2 feet (0.6 m). With the recommended bed width, or less, we can walk around the beds and easily tend to the plants. Since there is no need for footpaths in the bed, we can grow plants more closely together and increase food production from the space.

Right: A combination of various-sized wood-framed beds, black sunken repurposed nursery pots, and flower boxes creates tons of planting opportunities.

A mix of high-sided metal raised beds have been used to expand Gary's fruit garden.

Budget Saver #3:
Wander the Aisles of
Big Box Stores for Supplies

Don't make garden centers your first stop for supplies and other needs. You can find materials for building beds and trellises at big box stores for a better price. You just need to use your creative eye. Fire rings can be used as low-sided round raised beds. Wire closet shelving can be used for trellising. Plastic PVC piping and rebar can be used to build low tunnels. Clear painter's tarps can be used to cover the low tunnels or used for emergency frost protection. Wire for electric fencing has multiple purposes in a garden, and the spools are relatively inexpensive. The stone, brick, and construction areas of these stores are a gold mine for repurposing materials such as concrete mesh, rebar, and cinder blocks, and very often supplies like fencing and chicken wire are more reasonably priced.

Raised beds can be constructed from a wide range of different materials such as wood, bricks, cinder blocks, repurposed fire rings, old animal water troughs, feed containers, or any other material that creates a framed growing area. While many raised beds are directly open to the ground, if what you are using has a closed bottom, just remember to add drainage holes. If you are building with wood, you can create triangles, hexagons, or even stars, and metal raised beds come in squares, rectangles, circles, and ovals. Raised beds can be assembled to make a giant U shape where the inside space can be a sitting area or another type of food garden.

You can even layer raised beds on top of each other. For example, a 4-foot (1.2-m) square as the base, a 3-foot (1-m) square centered on top of that, and a 2-foot (0.6-m) square centered on top of that creates a beautifully tiered growing space similar to an herb spiral design. Each tier can be planted with different edibles such as herbs, vegetables, and edible flowers, and a dwarf fruit tree or berry bush can even be planted on top.

This top-down view of a planted herb spiral shows the structure off beautifully.

HERB SPIRALS

An herb spiral is a small garden built in a raised coil shape. This design was popularized by permaculture designer Bill Mollison and inspired by the spiral shape that is so commonly found in nature. In addition to saving space by having a vertical element, the benefits of an herb spiral include:

Aesthetics—Spirals throughout nature attract people's attention—from ferns to seashells to sunflower seedheads. The herb spiral adds visual interest to a garden, with its stone verticality and wide range of annual and perennial herb plants, much like a living sculpture.

Microclimates—The shape of this garden allows different herbs to receive their preferred levels of sunlight and water based on where they are located around the spiral. The top of the garden provides a slightly different microclimate than the bottom of the garden.

Access—The round shape of the herb spiral makes it easy to access all sides for planting, harvest, and care. Additionally, because this is such a compact garden design, it can be placed right outside your kitchen door, even on a patio or deck, making it more likely that the herbs will be used.

Maintenance—Many herbs are perennial and return to the garden every year, making this a low-maintenance garden. The longer herbs have been growing, the less water and care they require. Additionally, the stones or bricks used to build the spiral absorb the sun's warmth and act as an insulator, helping the soil retain heat during the colder months, which extends the growing season. The vertical shape of the garden also allows for water conservation as the water applied to the top filters its way down through the spiral.

Where to Build an Herb Spiral

There are two primary considerations when choosing the location for your herb spiral: sun and proximity. Most herbs are sun-loving, so choose a location for your herb spiral that receives at least 6 hours of direct sun per day throughout the growing season. Consider the impact of shade from trees as they leaf out. If your goal for the herb spiral is to provide easy access to garden-fresh herbs for your kitchen, place it as close to your kitchen as possible.

How to Build an Herb Spiral

The typical dimensions of an herb spiral are 6 feet (2 m) wide and 3 to 4 feet (about 1 m) high in the center. While most herb spirals begin directly on the ground, this design can be further elevated by building it on a platform for easy access for those with mobility issues. The other core design decision is what to use for the hard structure that contains the soil. Use what you have on hand or can find available for reuse in your community, or purchase materials that fit your aesthetic interests. Bricks, pavers, natural stones, a collection of smaller stones wrapped in a cage of chicken wire, or even logs make viable choices.

The materials needed for this garden (plants excluded) include:

Weed barrier—The base of the location for your herb spiral should be sheet mulched, or you can lay down gravel or landscape cloth—something that creates a barrier to weeds but drains well.

Measuring tools—String, a stake, and a measuring tape are useful for laying out the circular form of the structure if you are looking for a precise shape. Or take a more organic approach and allow the garden to take on an oval shape.

Hard structure—Gather sufficient stone or other materials needed to create the spiral shape, ensuring it is able to hold the soil in place.

Soil—Herbs typically prefer a sandier, well-draining soil. For the center and middle of the spiral, the height can be filled with layers of organic matter such as compost, straw, leaves, and grass clippings.

Garden tools—Gardening gloves, shovels and trowels, and a wheelbarrow help in your garden-building process.

STEP-BY-STEP PROCESS FOR BUILDING YOUR HERB SPIRAL

1.	Place the stake at the center of your planned herb spiral location and attach the string after cutting it to be about a yard (meter) long. This creates a spiral with a 6-foot (2-m) diameter. Use this to mark the spiral's shape on the ground; you can use chalk, a stick, or even spray paint if helpful.
2.	Cover the area with your selected weed barrier.
3.	Place your hard material (bricks, stones, etc.), starting at the outside and circling in. Leave space open at the end of the circle to be the start of your ramp for the spiral, coiled like a nautilus shell.
4.	Once you have done 360 degrees of your first level, it's time to add your first layers of mulch, compost, and soil.
5.	Create the incrementally increasing height of the spiral using a two across, one up ratio and add in more organic matter and soil as you go. Herbs do not need a deep soil layer.

This simple herb spiral at Freetown Farm is made from rocks found on-site. It was simple to build and plant.

How to Plant an Herb Spiral

When deciding which herbs to plant and where to plant them in your spiral, first consider their sunlight and water needs. The herbs that require more sun and less water should be planted closer to the top of your spiral. Mediterranean herbs such as marjoram, oregano, rosemary, and thyme are a good choice for the top of the herb spiral since they like it hot and dry. The east side of the herb spiral is ideal for more delicate plants that enjoy morning sun and more water, for example parsley, cilantro, and chives. On the southwest side, herbs such as basil, lavender, and sage thrive. Plant the more water-loving herbs closer to the bottom of the spiral. Those that prefer more shade will be happiest on the north side.

Right: This beautiful herb spiral at Freetown Farm is an efficient use of space, allowing easy access to a greater number of plants.

KEYHOLE GARDEN

A keyhole garden is a raised circular bed that has a walkway into the center, where a compost bin is built in. This design is great for people with small spaces, in areas where the soil is sub-optimal, and for people who have mobility constraints that make low-to-the-ground gardening difficult.

The height of the garden bed is flexible, the path into the center makes the whole garden easy to reach, and the compost bin serves as a convenient and efficient place to put yard and kitchen waste and put it right to work fertilizing the surrounding plants.

The following are the essential steps to building a keyhole garden:

- **Choose your location:** The ground should be level and not prone to holding water. Consider the amount of sun you will need for what you want to grow. Since you will be bringing compost to this garden, a location that is convenient for your kitchen or yard scraps creates efficiency.
- **Determine your design:** Stones are commonly used to create keyhole gardens, but you can be creative and use bricks, wood, or anything else that will allow you to get the height (typically 2 to 3 feet [0.6 to 1 m]) and soil containment you need. Similarly, a circle is the traditional shape, but you can go with an oval, square, octagon, etc., as long as there is a pathway (usually about 24 inches [60 cm] wide) to the compost in the center. Keyhole gardens should be no larger than 6 feet (2 m) in diameter so you can easily reach everything. The compost cage in the center of the keyhole should be made out of something like chicken wire to hold the compost in but allow water to flow out of the cage and into the garden— stakes will help hold the cage in place.
- **Fill the growing bed:** Use a quality gardening soil (see chapter 7 for some options to fill the bed), creating a slight grade so the soil slopes away from the compost cage. If the material you used for the walls of the bed has gaps, you can use cardboard to line the interior before you add the soil. Inside the compost cage you should put 3 to 5 inches (8 to 13 cm) of rocks or gravel to allow for the aeration that supports decomposition. Over the rocks, simply fill the cage to the top with layers of kitchen scraps and yard waste.
- **Plant your garden:** What you choose to plant depends on what you and your family want to eat. That said, good choices for this kind of garden include leafy greens, tomatoes, onions, strawberries, herbs, and root veggies that like non-compacted soil, such as carrots. Add mulch around the base of the plants to help the soil stay moist.
- **Maintain your garden:**
  - Water your keyhole garden directly into the compost cage, allowing water to flow through the compost and spread nutrients into your garden.
  - Add yard and kitchen scraps when the level of compost in the cage drops below the level of the soil in the garden.
  - Change the type or placement of your crops each year to support the health of the soil and your plants.
  - Check the garden each spring for any repairs that are needed. The compost cage should be cleaned out and restarted every several years.

Left: A food forest in progress at Freetown Farm. We are sheet mulching along the edge of established fruit tree saplings in the fall in preparation for adding a lower layer including blueberries, comfrey, and asparagus in the spring.

Right: This food forest at Gary's homestead consists of layers of edible plants, from trees all the way down to groundcovers. This shows a medicinal plant (echinacea) and edibles like apples, sunflowers, and herbs.

FOOD FOREST

A food forest is a diverse crop of edible plants, planted following basic guidelines found in forest growth. This includes trees, fruits, berries, flowers, roots, herbs, vegetables, and fungi. Taller plants like fruit trees are often placed with a strategy to use their canopy and moving shadow for plants that prefer less sun. Shade-loving plants with shallower root systems find the perfect conditions to flourish under tree canopies. Mid-sized plants and bushes that prefer more sun find homes along the edges of the food forest and in open pockets of sunshine. Food forests are great places to incorporate climbing plants such as grapes or kiwi vines. Placement is based on understanding plants' needs and growing habits. Smaller plants and sprawling vining plants find places along the ground, around the edges of walking paths, and between taller food-producing companions. Generally speaking, there is an upper level, middle level, ground level, root level, and a level for edible mushrooms. Mushrooms are often overlooked in edible gardens, but they adapt extremely well to shaded areas. It is this combination of levels that creates a food forest in any yard.

THE SEVEN LAYERS OF A FOOD FOREST GARDEN

1. Canopy = large fruit and nut trees
2. Low Tree Layer = dwarf fruit-bearing trees
3. Shrub or Bush Layer = fruit-producing shrubs
4. Herbaceous Layer = most "classic" vegetable crops
5. Rhizosphere = crops with edible roots
6. Groundcover Layer = low-growing edible plants
7. Vining Layer = crops that climb up other plants

Gary's friend Sofi truly transformed what was once a grassy area into an edible landscape with many layers of plants.

A true food forest is often created on a large scale and becomes an actual self-sustaining forest ecosystem, but you can adapt it to fit smaller spaces and maintain the principles of the design. Perhaps you have enough land to let your food forest mature with 25-, 40-, even 100-foot (8- to 30-m)-tall nut and fruit trees. The tallest trees in a food forest are known as the canopy, upper canopy, or overstory. They provide food—though hard to reach—but also provide shade and leaves to nourish the forest floor. And they define the growing landscape. Indigenous

communities around the world have planted and maintained large, community-tended food forests for centuries.

On a smaller scale, the design principles remain essentially the same, and they can be incorporated into most garden settings. It is important to use the 7 layers in your design to best maximize food production. However, the true canopy layer of the largest trees can be omitted or shifted to open space where other plants won't be impacted by the shade. A 40-foot (12-m) nut tree can cast a lot of shade, preventing sunlight from reaching your other gardens. In smaller-scale food forests, consider using smaller dwarf and semi-dwarf trees that only grow to be 10 to 25 feet (3 to 8 m) high. Once the trees are in, you can start adding smaller diversified edible plants, in layers, with the goal of learning how to replicate and maintain a more natural ecosystem.

One of the biggest barriers is getting over-whelmed and not starting your journey of building an edible landscape. The food forest is a great project to take in slow stages. For example, in year one you can plant the canopy of smaller fruit trees, year two you can add shrubs and bushes and herbaceous vege-table crops. In year three you can work on developing the rhizosphere and planting groundcover food crops. Then in year four you can add vining crops and mushrooms. In this way, over time, you can expand your food forest, maximize the space for production, and make it more self-sustaining.

One of Gary's small-scale food forests is shown here and uses key principles of the food-forest planting technique.

INCLUDE BOTH PERENNIALS AND ANNUALS IN YOUR EDIBLE LANDSCAPE

Take the long view on growing an edible landscape and reduce the amount of planting work you need to do each year by emphasizing the use of perennial plants. Perennial plants include fruit and nut trees, most berries, many herbs, and a fairly large number of vegetables, depending on your growing climate. These plants are great additions because they come back year after year and therefore can anchor some of your edible landscape design. You can plant some perennials from seed, but many of them take several years before they start to produce, so putting in transplants or saplings will hasten the harvest. Buying from a local nursery is a good choice because the plants are more likely to be adapted to your weather conditions and soil.

Once you have your most substantive perennials placed, you can start companion planting. For example, place onions and chives under young trees to prevent digging pests and disease, or plant native flowers to attract pollinators. These companion plants can also be perennials (see the table on page 114 for a more comprehensive list of perennial plants). For the first few years of your garden, at least, annuals will likely be an important part of your food-growing goals. They can fill the space as your perennials grow, and many of the most-loved edible plants are annuals (tomatoes, peppers, peas, squash, many leafy greens, etc.), so they will have pride of place in many edible landscapes. Edible flowers, both perennial and annual, are great to incorporate into your design as well. For example, sunflowers are a fun choice for filling space because they are low maintenance, and you can chop and drop their large stalks at the end of the growing season to add nutrients back into the soil.

Perennials and annuals are planted in a garden by the house.

Sofi incorporated some of the principles of a small-scale food forest into her design.

Containers are used in spaces, fruit vines creep across the ground, and food plants are everywhere.

Based on our climates, different fruit and nut trees will be available for growing. Some trees like heat and are damaged by freezing temperatures. Some trees need a dormancy period of cold or freezing temperatures and won't produce fruit without this period. The best way to decide what to grow is by first identifying what food-bearing trees do well in your area. We recommend buying dwarf or semi-dwarf trees. Many trees are grafted onto a root stock that inhibits the growth of the canopy and therefore keeps a tree to a manageable height. Dwarf trees range in height from 8 to 12 feet (2.5 to 3.75 m). A semi-dwarf tree may grow 12 to 15 feet (3.75 to 4.5 m) tall. Without being grafted to rootstock, the trees may easily grow 30 to 50 feet (9 to 15.25 m), a height that would cast excessive shade and make tending and harvesting them practically impossible.

Planting dwarf fruit trees is easy, and though it takes several years before you'll receive an ample harvest, the wait is well worth it.

Dwarf fruit trees, such as this apple, are perfect for small and modest-sized edible landscapes.

Dwarf fruit trees are practical, and they produce really well as demonstrated by this peach tree.

Identify the location of the root stock and trunk graft; don't plant the tree any deeper than where they meet.

We recommend buying trees that are 3 years old or older when possible. They are more expensive, but you won't have to wait as long for them to produce. Trees are best planted in late winter, early spring, or mid-late fall. The cooler temperatures provide time for the tree's root system to establish before having to support a full canopy of leaves in the summer heat. When planting the trees, dig a hole that is twice as wide as the container. The depth of the hole should only be slightly above the height of the root ball. It is very important not to cover the graft where the trunk and root stock meet. It is easily visible when looking at the bottom of the tree trunk. If you cover over where the graft occurs, the tree will send out roots from the trunk and the tree will grow to full size. Water the tree well several times weekly for 8 to 12 weeks.

4

PLANNING AND GROWING FOR YOUR CONDITIONS

There is a world full of edible plants to grow, but they won't all thrive in every garden. Some plants are hardy to extremely low temperatures, while others prefer warmer conditions and are easily damaged by freezing temperatures. There are cool-weather plants that prefer cooler soil and air temperatures. Many of these plants can tolerate a frost or even deep freezes. Their leaves freeze and thaw without being damaged. Or, in the case of perennial plants and hardy trees and shrubs, they may go dormant during the colder months. Other edible plants are frost sensitive and are killed off by a touch of the briefest frost. These are the warm-weather herbs, flowers, and vegetables that prefer warmer soil and hotter days. Some gardens receive regular rain every month, while other gardens get very little rain each year. Sunlight levels vary from garden to garden too. Because of all this variation, it is important to understand your garden's growing conditions throughout the year. Doing so helps in developing a planting plan. The last thing you want to do is spend money and time on plants that don't like the conditions associated with your garden. This chapter provides a basic understanding of how your soil, temperature averages, rainfall, and sunlight affect the plants growing in your garden.

Left: If you choose edible plants that grow in your conditions, success is very likely.

Wine cap mushrooms are often overlooked as an option for an edible landscape area that has challenging conditions.

SOIL

It is important to understand that many methods of building garden beds will work. Some of these are described in chapter 3. Once the beds are established, you can decide on how you want to amend, fertilize, and tend the spaces on an ongoing basis. Most soil is good enough to start growing. Your soil will improve year after year as you work to improve it. And so will your skills. You don't need to have perfect soil to start, because plants grow in a wide range of soils and conditions. We believe in getting started and learning as you grow.

Efforts to improve soil can be focused on the top 4 to 6 inches (10 to 15 cm) of the soil surface. The soil below that depth will improve over time as roots and worms move through it. Worms will aerate the lower earth and leave behind beneficial castings. Roots systems will open spaces and decay in those spaces, easily traveling to depths of 2 to 3 feet (1 m). In many cases we recommend removing only the above-ground portion of plants at the end of the season and leaving the root systems in place to decay in the earth.

The ongoing removal of roots and turning the soil, after initially setting up the beds, are not necessary. As gardeners, we thoughtfully consider the many needs of the plants we want to grow, but we often overlook our own needs or time constraints. Reducing work and managing time is good for the gardener and his or her gardens. Without a happy gardener, you can't have happy plants. Soil amending can be simplified to help manage the work and the costs associated with building up the growing areas. Keep in mind most soil is good enough to get started the first year. If the space has grass and weeds growing in it, if you can sink a shovel into it with a firm push, if it drains fairly quickly after rains, and if you can squeeze it into a ball and the soil mostly holds together yet easily crumbles with some pressure, then it is good enough for garden plants. Native soil generally falls into five categories. Each category requires a specific approach to amending it in order to reach that "good enough" status. While we could say, "Add ample compost to the planting area and mix well to create a loose soil with high amounts of organic matter," we also know that that can be expensive and complicated. Compost is always king and should be used regularly when available. When it is not, here are some basic options to get started.

NO-FRILLS FIXES FOR FIVE SOIL TYPES

Basic Soil Type	Bed Types	Initial Preparation	Additional Preparation	Final Preparation
Little to No Topsoil	Containers, Raised Beds	N/A	Purchase containers and *basic garden soil. Build or purchase raised beds.	Use containers or raised beds with 24-inch (60-cm) sides. Fill with *basic garden soil.
Very Rocky	Containers, Raised Beds	Level for container placement or framed growing areas.	Purchase containers and *basic garden soil. Build or purchase raised beds.	Use containers or raised beds with 24-inch (60-cm) sides. Fill with *basic garden soil.
Heavy Clay	Containers, Raised Beds, Earth Beds	Remove unwanted plants and compost them. Using a shovel or spading fork, **loosen/aerate the heavy-clay growing area.	Amend the native earth with 4 to 6 inches (10 to 15 cm) of *basic garden soil for earth beds.	Work newly applied soil into the top 4 to 6 inches (10 to 15 cm) of heavy clay.
Heavy Sand (Not Common)	Containers, Raised Beds, Earth Beds	Remove unwanted plants and compost them.	Amend native earth with 6 inches (15 cm) of ***compost/basic garden soil for earth beds.	Work newly applied soil into the top 6 to 12 inches (15 to 30 cm) of heavy sand.
"Good Enough" (It is up to you how much you want to improve the earth beds to start.)	Containers, Raised Beds, Earth Beds	Remove unwanted plants. Amend and plant as you wish into earth beds.	You can use the cardboard method and add 2 to 4 inches (5 to 10 cm) of *basic garden soil for earth beds	If you want to greatly improve the earth beds, 2 to 4 inches (5 to 10 cm) of compost could be added.

*Basic gardening soil will vary based on where you live, how you buy it, or how you make it. It is basically a combination of organic matter, compost, peat moss, and earth. Local landscape companies often have a basic garden soil for building beds. It also comes as a bagged product and may be labeled as "garden soil." Bags labeled "container mix" or "potting mix" will work, but they are more expensive products.

**Loosen/aerate means sink in the fork tines or shovel blade 6 inches (15 cm) deep and gently lift the soil, but do not turn it, to create pockets of air space below the surface.

***Compost/basic garden soil should fill the top 4 to 6 inches (10 to 15 cm) of your new growing beds. When compost is available, all compost can be used in place of garden soil. Where compost is not available, a basic garden soil can be used. A 50/50 mix of both is best for new beds.

SEASONAL TEMPERATURES

Soil temperature and ambient temperature impact how plants grow. Your local last frost date in spring and first frost date in fall define the length of your growing season for both frost-tolerant, cool-weather crops and frost-sensitive, warm-weather crops. But the high temperatures in your area are equally as important to know as the frost dates when it comes to selecting which crops to grow.

For example, tomato and pepper plants love the warm weather, but they may abort flowers and even drop fruit when temperatures regularly pass 95°F (35°C). Because of this, in areas that have extremely hot summers, warm autumns, and very mild winters, it is sometimes best to plant tomatoes and peppers after the high-temperature period of summer has passed.

Cool-weather crops are plants that prefer cooler soil and air temperatures and can easily tolerate a frost. These plants grow and produce best before the heat of summer arrives.

If you don't typically get frost in your area, you most likely can grow many different food plants even through the winter. We cover specific plant varieties in chapter 7, along with the growing conditions preferred by each one.

As you can see, knowing the local average monthly day and night temperatures is essential to figuring out what you can grow over the season and when it should be planted into your edible landscape. An internet search can help you build a table similar to the one on page 99. In this table, we used historical weather data for Baltimore, Maryland, where we both live. You can search the following phrase to get this information for your home growing zone: "first and last frost date (your city) (your state or province)." If that search doesn't give you enough detail, you can add each specific month into the search. It only takes about 30 minutes to collect the data for this type of chart. Also note which months will have frosts and which months will have temperatures that cause the ground to freeze. Many seeds won't germinate until the upper 4 to 6 inches (10 to 15 cm) of soil regularly range above 50°F (10°C). In central Maryland, this period starts in late March with the warming temperatures, but fully arrives in mid-April with warm rains and warmer day temperatures.

The Garden Journal: An Essential Tool

There is a learning curve when it comes to growing food. Accept mistakes and enjoy your success. You really can only learn by doing. But don't let mistakes and successes slip your mind. Use a journal to track times you planted seeds, the last and first frost date of each year, and the dates pests or diseases showed up. Also note when temperatures get so hot that plants seem to shut down production. That might be a good time to bring out shade cloth to help protect your plants from the heat. Write down what you felt went wrong and what went right, noting the dates of the events. It is important to focus on the whole experience when planting your edible landscape. We often focus on the failures, but also write down varieties of plants that did extremely well or seemed resistant to diseases. Make a note of when the cold of winter rolled in to stay. A journal is an essential tool that will let you plan and plant better the following year.

Use a journal or log book to track the conditions and happenings in your garden. Keeping a record is an important step toward success.

Prematurely putting seeds and transplants into the cold ground leads to rotting seeds, struggling transplants, and disappointment.

Using the data in the table, you'll see that the primary growing season in our area is March through November. I can grow cool-weather crops in the spring and again in the fall. We have a solid 4 to 5 months (May through September) to grow warm-season crops. If we want to use low tunnels, cloches, or other ways to manage temperature changes, we can start the growing season a few weeks early. Using the same items, we can also extend the harvest period for certain crop types later into fall. We can use this information as a pretty good guideline for building planting and growing schedules.

This data chart is also used to figure out what fruit trees and bushes can grow where we live. For example, apple trees and other fruit trees and bushes need a specific number of chill hours (hours of cold temperatures below a specific threshold) to produce fruit each year (see sidebar, page 100). They can survive temperatures well below freezing when dormant. Our area meets the need for chill hours from December through March. Other fruit trees, like many citrus trees, need nonfreezing winters, so they would not be good candidates for our gardens.

In chapter 7 we will discuss seed starting and growing your own garden transplants. The last frost date is also used to figure out when to start different plant seed varieties indoors.

SAMPLE WEATHER TABLE FOR PLANTING SCHEDULE

SAMPLE CHART for Baltimore, Maryland, USA

Last Frost Date: April 30 – May 15   **First Frost Date:** October 7 – October 21

Month	Average Day Temp. °F (°C)	Average Night Temp. °F (°C)	Ground Freeze	Frost Risk	Cool Crops	Warm Crops	Special Instructions
January	43°F (6°C)	25°F (-4°C)	Yes	Yes	No	No	Start Seeds Indoors
February	46°F (8°C)	27°F (-3°C)	Yes	Yes	No	No	Start Seeds Indoors
March	55°F (13°C)	34°F (1°C)	Yes	Yes	Yes	No	Start Seeds Indoors
April	67°F (19°C)	44°F (7°C)	No	Yes	Yes	Maybe	Plant Protection
May	76°F (24°C)	53°F (12°C)	No	Yes	Yes	Yes	Beware of Late Frost
June	84°F (29°C)	63°F (17°C)	No	No	Yes	Yes	Finishing Harvest
July	89°F (32°C)	68°F (20°C)	No	No	No	Yes	Beware of High Temps
August	87°F (31°C)	66°F (19°C)	No	No	Maybe	Yes	Transplants, Direct Seed
September	80°F (27°C)	59°F (15°C)	No	No	Yes	Yes	Finishing Harvesting
October	68°F (20°C)	47°F (8°C)	No	Yes	Yes	Maybe	Plant Protection
November	57°F (14°C)	37°F (3°C)	No	Yes	Yes	Maybe	Plant Protection
December	48°F (9°C)	30°F (-1°C)	Yes	Yes	Maybe	No	Plant Protection

Watering your edible landscape effectively, whether by hand or using an automated system, is essential, especially as your plants establish.

RAINFALL AND WATERING

The required growing temperatures may be met in your locality, but is there enough rain to support plant growth? Generally speaking, to have a diversity of food-producing plants, the garden will need to receive water at least a couple times a week, with one of these times being a deep soaking. A deep soaking means enough water to seep down a solid 12 inches (30 cm) into the garden beds. Very often we only water the shallow roots in the upper part of the soil. The water can come from natural rainfall if you live in an area where it consistently rains several times a month. But usually, rain needs to be supplemented with hand-watering. Even in reasonably rainy Maryland, if we want our plants to flourish, we have to water with a hose several times weekly during the high heat of summer.

Unfortunately, there is no chart that tells you how often to water or when to water. The general rule of thumb is less often when plants are small and temperatures are cool, more often when plants are growing and it is warmer, and very often when plants are tall and it is hot. Rain only counts if it is a soaking rain that gets into the depth of the soil.

Designing the garden in a way that conserves moisture—typically through mulching and incorporating native food plants—and efficiently moves water to all the areas will save resources. Smaller gardens can often be hand-watered with a smaller hose. Larger gardens spread across a property may require setting up sprinkler systems or using longer hoses. In areas where water access is limited, a drip irrigation system with a timer may be required.

Watering is more important when plants are first seeded or transplanted. Based on conditions, watering

Chill Hours for Fruit-Bearing Trees and Bushes

It is so exciting to think about what you want to grow, but you have to understand the needs of your plants to ensure they produce year after year. Chill hours are temperatures between 32°F (0°C) and 45°F (7°C). You may need as little as 100 hours or as much as 1,000 hours based on the variety of the fruit tree or berry bush. Keep in mind the hours do not count if temperatures are below freezing. You can look up chill hours for fruit-bearing canes (like raspberries or blackberries), bushes, or trees easily. Chill hours do not have to be consecutive, but they do have to occur cumulatively when the plants are in their dormant stage.

every other day for the first couple of weeks is not unrealistic in order to help the new plants grow roots that reach deeper into the soil.

A detailed discussion on irrigation is beyond the scope of this book. The best way to find out your watering needs is to ask locally. Most gardeners love to help, share information, and show off their gardens. Look online for a local gardening group and ask them about what they are growing and which edible plants are native and adapted to the local rainfall. Finding someone local who has successfully addressed an issue you encounter is always golden.

Both sides of this fence, and the inner space beyond it, all have different growing conditions. Plants will be selected based on the unique growing conditions of each site.

SUNLIGHT

It's important to know the amount of sunlight each plant needs to photosynthesize and thrive. Plants generally fall into the categories of full sun (6 to 8 or more hours), partial sun (4 to 6 hours), partial shade (2 to 4 hours), and shade (diffused sunlight). To further complicate things, several hours of morning sun is not as potent as a couple hours of midafternoon sun. In the picture at top right, you can see a peach tree and blackberry canes. Though the photo shows mostly sun, this area is normally well divided between sun and shade. One side of the fence gets mostly shade, and the other side gets mostly sun. These beds are ready for plants that have requirements this space provides.

Chapter 2 suggested observing the sun and noticing where it falls throughout your property. Pick the sunniest area for sun-loving crops, pick the areas of shade for the shade-loving crops, and the rest of the space can be tested out with plants that need something in between. Many of the charts and menus we have throughout the book will identify the amount of sun a particular plant needs. Chapters 5 and 6 highlight many edible plants that thrive in different conditions in terms of temperature, moisture, and sunlight.

The entrance to the youth garden at Freetown Farm is in full southern exposure overall, but has a variety of micro-exposures based on fencing, root pouches, and structural shade.

5

COMMON
AND UNCOMMON
EDIBLE PLANTS

When people think about edible landscapes, most will conjure up a vision of classic vegetable gardens and the tomatoes, cucumbers, and leafy greens found in the rows and beds. This chapter is intended to help you think beyond standard vegetable gardening. We will review ten plant families that share basic characteristics and contain most of our edible plants. The most common vegetable garden plants grown globally are summarized here, but we would like to emphasize less commonly known edible flowers, bushes, herbs, vines, trees, perennial plants, and wild plants often thought of as "weeds." Ten in-depth plant profiles, one for each plant family, will supplement charts that introduce sixty plants we hope you will consider in the creation of your own edible landscapes!

Left: This edible landscape view is filled with a surprising number of edible plants. Strawberries, lovage, oregano, and even tulips, whose petals are edible.

PLANT IDENTIFICATION

The ability to identify a plant is very important for people interested in harvesting edible plants from the wild or their yard or garden. This is especially true when harvesting plants that have non-edible look-alikes. We recommend using a botanical field guide with clear photographs to properly identify plants before harvesting them. The introduction to any reputable guide should offer plenty of tips on how to recognize the various features of each unique plant. Always use multiple features of a plant to determine its identity, instead of relying on a single feature, because the overall themes do not always apply to every plant.

PLANT FAMILIES

Every plant belongs to a botanical family. Most of the plants in the same family have similar characteristics and requirements, which is helpful when thinking about what edible plants will be a good fit for your preferences and space availability. The following are ten plant families that are highly (but not always entirely) edible. The table is organized alphabetically by the plant family's Latin scientific name since some common names vary regionally. **PLEASE BE SURE TO ONLY eat plants, and parts of plants, that you are completely sure of both in terms of official edibility and your own personal compatibility with the plant.**

Edible landscapes can be so beautiful! This planting contains bee balm, edible allium flowers, and oregano, combined with ornamental plants.

Family	Edible Examples	Characteristics	Needs
Amaranth Amaranthaceae ~2,500 species	Beets, quinoa, **celosia**, chard, spinach, lamb's quarters, amaranth, Inca wheat	Flowering plants, mostly herbs and subshrubs, distributed throughout most of the world. Annuals or perennials. The plant has simple leaves that are sometimes succulent or hairy and are usually arranged alternately along the stems. The stems, roots, and leaves are often red because of the presence of betalain pigments.	Commonly grown in saline soils. Cool-season vegetables, well-drained soil and compost, non-acidic soil, deep watering
Onion Amaryllidaceae, subfamily Allioideae, formerly family Alliaceae ~1,600 species	Onion, **walking onion,** garlic, leek, chive	Plants have bulbs or underground stems, several lance-shaped leaves that are grouped at the base of the stem or arranged alternately, and flowers that have three or six sepals and petals.	Grown throughout the world, mostly in the temperate zones. Warm-season, needs loamy soil, needs to stay moist
Parsley Apiaceae over 3,000 species, some edible, some deadly	Fennel, celery, carrot, parsnip, parsley, coriander, fennel, celery, anise, chervil, **cilantro/coriander,** cum-in, caraway, dill	Mostly white or yellow flowers that look like upturned double umbrellas starting from a single point on a long main stem.	Slow germinating, cool-season, needs well-drained soil
Aster Asteraceae more than 19,000 species	Lettuce, artichoke, calendula, sunflower, **dandelion,** endive, salsify, safflower	Flowering plants including herbs, shrubs, and trees distributed throughout the world. Composite flowers, where one flowerhead is com-posed of many smaller flowers on a single disk. Each small flower has five petals. Grows fast, shallow roots, attracts pollinators	Cool-season or in shade of larger plants, needs lots of organic matter
Mustard Brassicaceae ~3,200 species, many edible	Broccoli, cabbage, cauliflower, **kale,** many mustards, bok choi, radish, arugula, brussels sprouts, collards, turnip, rutabaga	Simple leaves with cross shape. Notable flower structure—four sepals, four petals, six stamen, one pistil	Comfortable in bare, sparse ground. Short life cycles and quick growing. Prefer cool weather, needs pH-balanced soil

Family	Edible Examples	Characteristics	Needs
Gourds Cucurbitaceae ~950 species	Cucumber, melon, squash, **pumpkin,** zucchini, gourd	Mostly fast-growing annual vines. Commonly have large yellow or white flowers, large and lobed leaves, and hairy stems.	Needs moisture, but not too wet, needs lots of compost
Pea Fabaceae (formerly Leguminosae) more than 19,000 species, some mildly poisonous	Peas, peanuts, pinto beans, lima beans, soybeans, cow peas, black-eyed peas, chickpeas, lentils, garbanzo beans, licorice, jicama, **scarlet runner beans**	Characterized by compound leaves and the production of fruits called legumes. Irregular flowers with unique petals called a banner, wings, and keel. Plants range in size and can be in the form of trees, shrubs, vines, and herbs.	Distributed world-wide. Nitrogen fixing, relatively easy to grow in rich, well-draining soil.
Mint Lamiaceae more than 3,500 species	Mint, peppermint, rosemary, **sage,** thyme, oregano, basil, lavender, marjoram, savory	Square stems, opposite leaves, aromatic, spreads easily, often perennial	Drought tolerant once established, not too sensitive to soil conditions
Rose Rosaceae ~2,500 species	Rose hips, strawberries, **blackberries,** raspberries, apples, apricots, cherries, nectarines, peaches, plums	Generally woody plants, mostly shrubs or small to medium-sized trees, some of which are armed with thorns. Characterized by flowers with sepals and five petals, usually with numerous stamens. The leaves are oval shaped and have serrated edges.	Need a minimum of 6 hours of sun per day. Morning sun is especially important because it dries the leaves, which helps prevent diseases.
Nightshade Solanaceae ~2,700 species, some highly toxic	Tomato, eggplant, pepper, potato, gooseberries, **goji berries,** paprika, tomatillo	Ranges from annual and perennial herbs to vines, shrubs, and trees. The leaves are generally simple and alternately arranged. The flowers are usually conspicuous and solitary or clustered, with five sepals, petals, and stamens.	Found throughout the world but most abundant in tropical regions. Needs rich, well-composted soil, needs to stay damp

*The specific edible plant bolded and italicized for each plant family has a full profile provided at the end of this chapter. As you will see in our specific plant tables below, there are many more plant families in the world than featured here. If you are interested in a plant family that is listed below and not featured above, take the time to learn more about it. One great plant choice might inspire other related plants that you will enjoy growing and eating.

Parsley

Pumpkin

Onions

Sunflowers

Mustard

A small front-yard edible landscape contains such offerings as apples, strawberries, lavender, and parsley.

Oats are an example of an edible member of the grass family, along with rice, rye, and wheat.

Grass

As described in chapter 1, grass is not, in and of itself, a bad thing. The grass family (Poaceae) has more than 10,000 species, almost all of which have edible seeds. Grasses comprise staple food crops such as wheat, oats, corn, rice, barley, millet, rye, and even sugarcane. Grasses are monocots (single leaf, straight-veined leaves), ranging in size from yard grass to bamboo. They are wind pollinated, so their flowers aren't showy, but they do have reproductive parts enclosed in modified leaves called bracts.

CLASSIC GARDEN VEGETABLES

The following table features the fifteen most popular vegetable plants grown in gardens around the world. While these are classic vegetables, you can branch out by choosing less common varieties of many of these plants to explore and enjoy. Different varieties may be better in your particular geographic area.

Vegetable (and Family)	Crop Type	Ideal Sun Exposure	Frost Tolerant	Planting Temperatures & Best Method
Beans Pea family, Fabaceae	Warm-season	8+ hours	No	60°F–70°F (15°C–21°C) Direct Seeding
Broccoli Mustard family, Brassicaceae	Cool-season	8+ hours	Yes	50°F–60°F (10°C–15°C) Plant Transplants
Cabbage Mustard family, Brassicaceae	Cool-season	8+ hours	Yes	50°F–60°F (10°C–15°C) Plant Transplants
Carrots Parsley family, Apiaceae	Cool-season	8+ hours, but 6 hours will work	Yes	50°F–60°F (10°C–15°C) Direct Seeding
Cucumbers Gourd family, Cucurbitaceae	Warm-season	8+ hours	No	60°F–70°F (15°C–21°C) Direct Seeding or Transplants
Eggplants Nightshade family, Solanaceae	Warm-season	8+ hours	No	65°F+ (18°C+) Direct Seeding or Transplants
Garlic Onion family, Amaryllidaceae	Cool-season	8+ hours	Yes	Plant Cloves Planting Times Vary
Kale Mustard family, Brassicaceae	Cool-season Warm-season	8+ hours	Yes	45°F –55°F (7°C–13°C) Plant Transplants 55°F–60°F (13°C–16°C) Direct Seeding
Lettuce Aster family, Asteraceae	Cool-season	6+ hours	Yes	45°F–55°F (7°C–13°C) Plant Transplants 55°F–60°F (13°C–16°C) Direct Seeding
Onions Onion family, Amaryllidaceae	Cool-season	10+ hours, but 8 hours will work	Yes	45°F–55°F (7°C–13°C) Plant Transplants 55°F–60°F (13°C–16°C) Direct Seeding

Vegetable (and Family)	Crop Type	Ideal Sun Exposure	Frost Tolerant	Planting Temperatures & Best Method
Peas Pea family, Fabaceae	Cool-season	8+ hours, but 6 hours will work	Yes	45°F–55°F (7°C–13°C) Plant Transplants 55°F–60°F (13°C–16°C) Direct Seeding
Peppers Nightshade family, Solanaceae	Warm-season	8+ hours	No	65°F+ (18°C+) Direct Seeding or Transplants
Radishes Mustard family, Brassicaceae	Cool-season	8+ hours, but 6 hours will work	Yes	40°F–50°F (4°C–10°C) Direct Seeding
Spinach Amaranth family, Amaranthaceae	Cool-season	8+ hours, but 6 hours will work	Yes	40°F–50°F (4°C–10°C) Plant Transplants 50°F–60°F (10°C–16°C) Direct Seeding
Tomatoes Nightshade family, Solanaceae	Warm-season	8+ hours	No	60°F–70°F (16°C–21°C) Direct Seeding or Transplants

Green Peas

Bell Pepper

Spinach

Burgundy beans

Broccoli

Cabbage

Carrots

Radish

Kale

Tomatoes

Eggplant

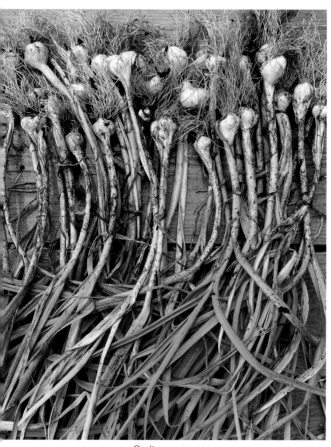

Garlic

Cucumbers

EXCITING ADDITIONS TO THE EDIBLE LANDSCAPE

To expand your horizons beyond the fifteen most common edible plants people grow around the world, the table below lists sixty specific edible plants. These represent a wide variety of plant families and a diversity of plant types that thrive in different growing conditions. Some plants might be annual in some geographic areas and perennial in others. The plant type column will help you make choices about layers of a food forest or other garden design elements.

Name and Plant Family	Annual / Perennial	Plant Type and Special Notes	Sun Exposure	Planting Temperature & Best Method
Apple Rose family, Rosaceae	Perennial	Tree, edible flower, leaves, and fruit, pollinator+	8 hours	50°F+ (10°C+) Direct seeding
Apricot Rose family, Rosaceae	Perennial	Vegetable	6+ hours	60°F+ (15°C+) Plant transplants 70°F–80°F (21°C–27°C) Direct seeding Seedlings should be exposed to a brief period below 50°F (10°C) to encourage bud set.
Artichoke Aster family, Asteraceae	Cool-season	8+ hours	Yes	50°F–60°F (10°C–15°C) Plant transplants
Asparagus Asparagus family, Asparagaceae	Perennial	Vegetable	8+ hours	70°F–85°F (21°C–29°C) Direct seeding 60°F–70°F (15°C –21°C) Plant transplants
Basil Mint family, Lamiaceae	Either	Herb, companion plant	6–8 hours	50°F–70°F (10°C–21°C) Direct seeding
Bee Balm Mint family, Lamiaceae	Perennial	Flower, edible flower, pollinator+	6+ hours	60°F+ (15°C+) Plant transplants
Blackberry* Rose family, Rosaceae	Perennial	Vine, pollinator+, young stems and leaves are edible	8+ hours	50°F+ (10°C+) Plant transplants
Blueberry Heath family, Ericaceae	Perennial	Shrub, edible fruit	6–10 hours	32°F–45°F (0°C–7°C) Plant transplants in late fall
Bok Choi* Mustard family, Brassicaceae	Annual or Biennial	Vegetable	3–5 hours	55°F–65°F (13°C–18°C) Plant transplants or direct seeding
Borage Borage family, Boraginaceae	Annual	Herb, edible flower, companion plant, pollinator+	6–8 hours	55°F–75°F (13°C–24°C) Direct seeding

Name and Plant Family	Annual / Perennial	Plant Type and Special Notes	Sun Exposure	Planting Temperature & Best Method
Bush Plums Rose family, Rosaceae	Perennial	Shrub, edible fruit, pollinator+	6+ hours	32°F–45°F (0°C–7°C) Plant transplants in late fall
Calendula Aster family, Asteraceae	Annual	Flower, edible flower, pollinator+	6–8 hours	55°F–65°F (13°C–18°C) Direct seeding
Celosia* Amaranth family, Amaranthaceae	Both	Flower, edible flower and leaves	6–8 hours	60°F–75°F (15°C–24°C) Plant transplants
Chamomile Aster family, Asteraceae	Either	Herb, flower, edible flower	4+ hours	45°F+ (7°C+) Plant transplants 60°F+ (15°C+) Direct seeding
Cherry Rose family, Rosaceae	Perennial	Tree, edible fruit and flower	6+ hours	43°F–58°F (6°C–14°C) Plant transplants
Chestnut, Sweet Beech family, Fagaceae	Perennial	Tree	4–8 hours. The tree grows fastest in partial sun but requires full sun to fruit.	70°F–80°F (21°C–27°C) Plant transplants
Chickweed Carnatian family, Caryophyllaceae	Annual	Wild, edible flower and leaves	4–8 hours	53°F–68°F (12°C–20°C) Direct seeding
Chicory Aster family, Asteraceae	Perennial	Wild, edible leaves and roots	6+ hours	65°F–70°F (18°C–21°C) Direct seeding or plant transplants
Chives Onion family, Amaryllidaceae	Perennial	Herb, edible flower and stems	6–8 hours	60°F–70°F (15°C–21°C) Direct seeding or plant transplants
Cilantro/ Coriander* Parsley family, Apiaceae	Annual	Herb, companion plant, pollinator+	4–6+ hours	55°F–70°F (13°C–21°C) Direct seeding
Citrus Rue family, Rutaceae	Perennial	Tree, edible flower	8+ hours	55°F–85°F (13°C–29°C) Plant transplants
Clover Pea family, Fabaceae	Perennial	Weed, edible flower	4–8 hours	45°F–65°F (7°C–18°C) Direct seeding
Currants Currant family, Grossulariaceae	Perennial	Shrub, edible flower and leaves	8+ hours	32°F–45°F (0°C–7°C) Plant transplants in late fall
Dandelion* Aster family, Asteraceae	Perennial	Weed, edible flower, pollinator+	6–10 hours but can tolerate less	50°F–80°F (10°C–27°C) Direct seeding

Name and Plant Family	Annual / Perennial	Plant Type and Special Notes	Sun Exposure	Planting Temperature & Best Method
Daylily* Lily family, Liliaceae	Perennial	Flower, edible flower, fast-growing, companion plant	4–6 hours	53°F–68°F (12°C–20°C) Plant transplants
Dill Parsley family, Apiaceae	Annual	Herb, companion plant, edible leaves, seeds, and flower	6–8 hours	60°F–70°F (15°C–21°C) Direct seeding
Elderberry Moschatel family, Adoxaceae	Perennial	Shrub/tree, edible flower	8+ hours, will tolerate less in heat	50°F+ (10°C+) Plant transplants
Figs Mulberry family, Moraceae	Perennial	Shrub, edible fruit and leaves	6+ hours	45°F+ (7°C+) Plant transplants 70°F–78°F (21°C–26°C) Propagate cuttings
Ginger Ginger family, Zingiberaceae	Perennial	Groundcover, edible, shade loving	2–5 hours	68°F–77°F (20°C–25°C) Direct seeding
Goji Berry* Nightshade family, Solanaceae	Perennial	Shrub, edible fruit	8+ hours	50°F+ (10°C+) Plant transplants
Grapes Grape family, Vitaceae	Perennial	Vine	7–8 hours	55°F–70°F (13°C–21°C) Plant transplants
Hardy Kiwi Chinese gooseberry family, Actinidiaceae	Perennial	Vine	6+ hours	55°F–65°F (13°C–18°C) Plant transplants
Hibiscus Mallow family, Malvaceae	Either	Shrub, edible flower	8+ hours	60°F–75°F (15°C–24°C) Plant transplants
Lamb's Quarters Amaranth family, Amaranthaceae	Annual	Wild, edible leaves	6–8 hours	50°F–78°F (10°C–26°C) Direct seeding
Lilacs Olive family, Oleaceae	Perennial	Shrub, edible flower	6–8 hours	32°F–45°F (0°C–7°C) Plant transplants in fall before first freeze
Mulberry Mulberry family, Moraceae	Perennial	Tree, edible fruit	4–8 hours	50°F–65°F (10°C–18°C) Plant transplants
Muscadine Grape family, Vitaceae	Perennial	Vine, edible fruit and leaves	6–8 hours	45°F–60°F (7°C–15°C) Plant transplants
Nasturtium Nasturtium family, Tropaeolaceae	Annual	Vining flower, companion plant, edible flower	6–8 hours is best, but 3–6 hours works	55°F–65°F (13°C–18°C) Direct seeding

Name and Plant Family	Annual / Perennial	Plant Type and Special Notes	Sun Exposure	Planting Temperature & Best Method
Okra Mallows family, Malvaceae	Perennial	Vegetable, edible flower	6–8 hours	70°F–85°F (21°C–29°C) Direct seeding or plant transplants
Oregano Mint family, Lamiaceae	Perennial	Herb, companion plant	6+ hours is best, but 4–6 hours works	60°F–80°F (15°C–27°C) Direct seeding or plant transplants
Passion Fruit Passion flower family, Passifloraceae	Perennial	Vine, edible flower	6+ hours is best, but 4–6 hours works	70°F–80°F (21°C–27°C) Plant transplants
Pawpaw Custard apple family, Annonaceae	Perennial	Tree, edible fruit	6 hours, requires filtered sun for the first year of life	75°F–85°F (24°C–29°C) Direct seeding
Pear Rose family, Rosaceae	Perennial	Tree, edible fruit	6–8 hours	50°F+ (10°C+) Plant transplants
Persimmon Ebony family, Ebenaceae	Biennial	Tree, edible fruit	6–8 hours	55°F–65°F (13°C–18°C) Plant transplants
Pines & Spruce Pine family, Pinaceae	Perennial	Wild, edible tips	6–8 hours	60°F+ (15°C+) Plant transplants
Purslane Purslane family, Portulacaceae	Annual	Wild, edible leaves, stem, and flower	6–8 hours	60°F+ (15°C+) Direct seeding
Raspberry Rose family, Rosaceae	Perennial	Vine, edible leaves and root	6–8 hours, slowly acclimate new plants to the sun	32°F–45°F (0°C–7°C) Plant transplants in late fall
Rhubarb Buckwheat family, Polygonaceae	Perennial	Vegetable	6+ hours	60°F–75°F (15°C–24°C) Plant transplants or direct seeding
Rose Rose family, Rosaceae	Perennial	Shrub, edible flower, bud, and hip	4+ hours	40°F–60°F (4°C–15°C) Plant transplants
Rosemary Mint family, Lamiaceae	Perennial	Herb, companion plant	6–8 hours	60°F–65°F (15°C–18°C) Plant transplants 70°F–75°F (21°C–24°C) Direct seeding
Sage* Mint family, Lamiaceae	Perennial	Herb, companion plant, pollinator+	6–8 hours, but can tolerate 2–6 hours	60°F–70°F (15°C–21°C) Plant transplants 65°F–70°F (18°C–21°C) Direct seeding

Name and Plant Family	Annual / Perennial	Plant Type and Special Notes	Sun Exposure	Planting Temperature & Best Method
Scarlet Runner Bean* Pea family, Fabaceae	Annual	Vine, pollinator+	6+ hours	55°F–70°F (13°C–21°C) Direct seeding
Squash* Cucurbit family, Cucurbitaceae	Annual	Vine, pollinator+	6 hours	70°F–85°F (21°C–29°C) Direct seeding
Strawberries Rose family, Rosaceae	Perennial	Groundcover, edible flower	8–10 hours	60°F–80°F (15°C–27°C) Plant transplants
Sunflowers Aster family, Asteraceae	Annual	Flower, edible seeds, pollinator+	6–8 hours	70°F–75°F (21°C–24°C) Direct seeding
Sweet Potato Morning glory family, Convolvulaceae	Perennial	Vine, edible roots	6+ hours	60°F+ (15°C+) Plant slips
Thyme Mint family, Lamiaceae	Perennial	Herb, companion plant	6–8 hours	65°F–70°F (18°C–21°C) Direct seeding 70°F+ (21°C+) Plant transplants
Violets Violet family, Violaceae	Perennial	Herb, edible flower	8+ hours	65°F–80°F (18°C–27°C) Plant transplants
Walking Onion* Onion family, Amaryllidaceae	Perennial	Vegetable, edible flower	6–8 hours	60°F–70°F (15°C–21°C) Direct seeding or plant transplants
Wood Sorrel Wood sorrel family, Oxalidaceae	Perennial	Wild, edible leaves	6 hours	60°F–80°F (15°C–27°C) Direct seeding

*The plants with an asterisk are those that have a full plant profile at the end of this chapter.
+The plant types with a plus sign (+) indicate they are pollinator friendly.

Plants of the onion family

Fruits and flowers in the rose family

The picture illustrates companion planting, using marigolds with leafy greens.

COMPANION PLANTING

Mixing together a diverse range of annuals and perennials including flowers, fruits, and vegetables makes a garden healthier. That said, there are certain combinations of plants that can really boost productivity when planted together.

Companion plants are those that help one another grow and produce to their fullest potential in some or all of the following ways:

- **Soil Nutrients**—Putting plants together that have different soil nutrient needs can help reduce competition and support the overall health of the plants in a particular area. Plants such as peas and beans help draw nitrogen into the soil, making it more available for the plants that need it.

- **Soil Structure**—Plants with long taproots like parsnips and carrots can help alleviate soil compaction and help pull nutrients and water up from deeper layers of the soil.
- **Protection**—Too much wind or sun can damage younger or more fragile plants. Thoughtful companion planting can use taller plants to shelter smaller ones.
- **Natural Supports**—Plants and flowers that have strong, tall stems make great natural supports for climbing plants. For example, cucumbers and snap peas love growing up the stalks of sunflowers or corn.
- **Weed Prevention**—Companion plants that act as a groundcover make it harder for weeds to crop up around taller plants.

Marigolds are a popular companion plant in the vegetable garden.

The Three Sisters planting method combines corn, pole beans, and squash.

Corn, beans, and squash are probably the most popular companion plants, having been combined by indigenous communities for centuries. Corn acts as a natural support that beans climb, and the squash spreads out along the ground, providing a great groundcover. These three plants have positive relationships at the root level as well, boosting growth and production.

Popular companion plants for vegetables include:

- **Basil** is a natural protectant for tomato plants because it repels hornworms (dill does too). Basil is also a great companion plant for asparagus, beans, beets, bell peppers, cabbage, chili peppers, eggplant, marigolds, oregano, and potatoes.
- **Borage** also protects tomatoes from hornworms and is a great beneficial insect/pollinator attractor. Borage supports strawberries in having a strong yield.
- **Cilantro/Coriander** has a scent that repels aphids and carrot flies, making it a great overall companion plant.
- **Lavender** has a scent that confuses many pests, and the flowers attract pollinators.
- **Marigolds** help virtually any vegetable, making them one of the most popular companion plants, but they are particularly helpful for tomatoes because they repel the nematodes that attack the roots of the plant.
- **Mint** repels both ants and cabbage moths and is a great multi-purpose plant (although it spreads, so keeping it in containers is advised).
- **Nasturtiums** help prevent insects such as aphids from attacking other plants. Aphids love nasturtiums and will surround them instead of their neighboring plants. Beneficial insects also love nasturtiums.
- **Sage** can protect surrounding plants from cabbage moths.
- **Zinnias** attract ladybugs, which are known to control unwanted pests like cabbage flies.

Left: Zinnias and tomatoes

Blackberry

BOTANICAL OVERVIEW
Latin name: *Rubus fruticosus*
Plant family: Rosaceae

IDENTIFICATION The blackberry plant is a bramble with long, naturally thorny, spreading stems. The leaves are alternate (one leaf per node on alternate sides), deep green on top and lighter green on the bottom, and each leaf is made up of three to five oval leaflets with serrated edges. The flowers are a classic example of the rose plant family, with five petals, numerous stamens, and a sweet aroma that attracts pollinators. The flowers are typically white or slightly pinkish and present in the late spring to early summer before the fruits start to form. The blackberry itself starts out green, transitions to red (when it can be confused with a raspberry), and is a dark purple/black and up to 1 inch (2.5 cm) long by the time it is fully ripe. The ripe blackberry has a soft, white, edible core when you pick it, whereas raspberries have a hollow core when you pick them and remove the top.

FOOD AND NUTRITION People have been foraging blackberries for millennia, and it is still a joyful way to spend a day. Blackberries can be enjoyed right off the vine as a snack or a garnish to a summer salad and can be prepared as jams, jellies, pies, crumbles, ice creams, and even sweet vinegars, wines, and beers. Blackberries have long been used in traditional medicine because of their many health benefits. They are high in vitamins C and K, fiber, manganese, and antioxidants, which make them a go-to for nurturing overall well-being and brain health in particular.

ECOLOGICAL ROLE The leaves of the blackberry bramble are enjoyed by a variety of caterpillar species as well as mammals such as deer. The flowers provide a valuable source of food for many pollinators, including numerous types of bees and butterflies. The berries are eaten by various birds and mammals (fox, bear, etc.). These animals also spread the seeds, wild-planting blackberries in woodlands, fields,

hedges, etc. The fact that blackberries are naturally thorny (some cultivars are thornless) makes them a protective habitat for many animals. The blackberry bramble can be used to minimize soil erosion in disturbed areas and to create property boundaries.

CULTIVATION Homegrown blackberries put store-bought blackberries to shame and are well worth the effort. In the United States and the United Kingdom, the blackberry is native, which makes them very hardy. If you just want to snack on berries straight off the bush, one might be enough, but you can experiment with the different varieties and have an ample harvest for cooking and preserving. The four different varieties—erect, thorny, thornless, and trailing—make blackberries a good fit for many different locations. For example, you could choose a thornless variety that is erect and plant it against a sunny spot on a fence for kids to pick from. The blackberry plant itself is perennial, but the specific canes are usually biennial, which means they put out leaves in their first year and fruit in their second year before dying back to let new ones form. Prune back the dry canes that are no longer producing fruit. Blackberries are best planted in the spring in well-drained, rich, acidic soil with full sun. If you are planting multiple blackberries, you will need to space them 3 to 7 feet (1 to 2 m) apart depending on the variety you choose.

Bok Choi

BOTANICAL OVERVIEW
Latin name: *Brassica rapa*
Common names: Pak choi, Bak choi, Chinese cabbage
Plant family: Brassicaceae

IDENTIFICATION Bok choi grows in heads of crunchy leaves that range from 4 to 12 inches (10 to 30 cm) long. It is similar to swiss chard in texture and appearance; the leaves have bright-white stems and green tops. Ancient Chinese craftsmen were captivated by its shape and size, so they frequently used the plant as a subject for jade carvings.

FOOD AND NUTRITION Both the stems and leaves are edible, with a flavorful taste. They can be harvested a few leaves at a time or by the head. The heads should still be tender when harvested, and the leaves are best when crunchy. Bok choi can be chopped and sautéed then served on its own, in stir fries, or on top of a main course. It is also popular in soups, salads, and sandwiches. Bok choi will stay fresh for 1 to 2 weeks after harvest, but it can also be preserved through fermentation. It is the foundation of kimchi, a traditional Korean food. It can also be used in the European method to produce sauerkraut; these condiments are great on a variety of food from eggs to hot dogs.

Bok choi contains folate, beta-carotene, and vitamins C, E, B$_6$, and K. Uniquely, it also contains selenium, which can help detoxify some cancer-causing compounds and reduce inflammation.

ECOLOGICAL ROLE Bok choi dates back 3,500 years to China's fertile Yangtze River region—it was likely cultivated from a variety of native species. In the 1500s, Chinese scientist Li Shizhen wrote a book detailing all of its medical benefits. From there, it gained massive popularity across Asia. It was introduced to Europe and North America by Chinese immigrants who used it for cooking and to treat symptoms of illness. They are hardy in cold temperatures, providing people with much-needed nutrients in the winter months.

CULTIVATION Bok choi should be planted in an area that receives 3 to 5 hours of sun a day, although it can tolerate full sun. The plant needs to steadily absorb water and nutrients as it grows, so it should be planted in fertile soil that retains moisture while still draining properly. Adding compost or organic fertilizer will help to improve growth. Bok choy should receive about 1 inch (2.5 cm) of water a week—a drought will cause the flavor to become bitter and the texture to worsen. The plant can tolerate light frost. In fall, light frosts can improve taste, but in spring they instead cause early bolting. Flea beetles are a major pest that affects this plant; they are more active in the spring than in the fall. Row covers are the best preventative measure, while spinosad and other fungal agents containing *Beauveria bassiana* will cause the beetle to dry out and die.

Celosia

BOTANICAL OVERVIEW
Latin name: *Celosia argentea*
Common names: Cockscomb, mfungu, woolflowers
Plant family: Amaranthaceae

IDENTIFICATION Celosia plants come in a variety
of shapes and colors, from flame-like flourishes to
complex mounds that look like coral or the rooster's
comb. The kind you would want to include in your
garden have brightly colored (red, pink, purple,
yellow, and coral), long-lasting plumes that stick
out from the center of the foliage. The leaves are
typically green (sometimes with purple) and broad
and pointed, having lighter veins that start from the
central rib and move to the sides of the leaf. The
plant forms a fairly small shrub that has flowers
at the top, blooming in the summer and fall.

FOOD AND NUTRITION A member of the amaranth
plant family, celosia is grown as a food crop in
many parts of the world, including Africa, India,
and Asia, although it is typically considered to be
a decorative plant in the United States. Early in
the growing season, the stems, leaves, and young
flowers can all be harvested and prepared very similarly to spinach in a wide variety of cooked dishes.
Regular use of the leaves will encourage them to
continue to grow back for continued edible yield.
Both the taste and nutritional value of celosia are
better with young plants that have not gone into
full flower. Like other leafy greens, celosia is high
in iron, calcium, and vitamins A and C.

ECOLOGICAL ROLE The celosia plant flourishes
in warm climates around the world. It is a hardy
plant that does not require much water to thrive,
so it is an important part of the diet in a range of
places where the growing conditions are not ideal
for other more-sensitive crops. In addition to the
human benefit, the bright flowers of the celosia
plant, which are what make it a popular ornamental
selection for many gardeners, also make it a valuable
part of the ecosystem for pollinators such as bees,
butterflies, and hummingbirds.

CULTIVATION Celosia is a tender perennial in
warmer climates and an annual in cooler climates
that happily reseeds itself. It should be grown in
full sun, at least 6 to 8 hours a day, in well-drained,
nutrient-rich soil. More robust flower production
will be achieved with a liquid plant food applied
every couple of weeks. Celosia is very hardy and
grows well while other plants may succumb
to mold and mildew. Taller varieties, especially
the cockscomb, may benefit from being staked
for support.

Cilantro/Coriander

BOTANICAL OVERVIEW
Latin name: *Coriandrum sativum*
Plant family: Apiaceae

IDENTIFICATION Cilantro and coriander refer to the same plant. In North America, cilantro refers to the leaves and stalks of the plant, and the dried seeds are referred to as the spice coriander. Elsewhere, coriander is the name for the leaves, stalks, and seeds. This herb/spice is in the same plant family as carrots and dill and can be easily confused with parsley, which looks very similar.

FOOD AND NUTRITION The citrus-like flavor of the leaves is best before the plant flowers and goes to seed (bolts). After this happens, the leaves lose some of their classic lime-like flavor and become more bitter. Cilantro leaves are favored in soups and stews, dressings and sauces, rice dishes, salads, salsas, and a variety of zesty entrees. Cilantro leaves are best used fresh and at the very end of cooking because they lose their flavor after substantial heat exposure. While many people love cilantro, others have a strong negative taste reaction to it, thought to potentially be genetic, where the flavor comes through as soapy.

The coriander seed has a less controversial taste and aroma than the leaves. The ground spice still has a hint of citrus, which is mellowed by a nuttiness that is often combined with other spices such as cinnamon or cumin that have a warm flavor profile. Classic recipes that use coriander include curries, meat rubs, soups, stews, and rice dishes, as well as various pickles. The tender young green seeds are also delicious before they harden and can be pickled like capers or added to salsas.

Cilantro leaves have much higher levels of vitamins, such as A, K, and E, but lower levels of minerals (the leaves are 92 percent water). The coriander seeds have lower levels of vitamins, but far more minerals, such as manganese, iron, magnesium, and calcium.

ECOLOGICAL ROLE The flowers of the cilantro/coriander plant are open and lay in flat heads called umbels, making them accessible to a wide range of pollinator species. You can expect the clusters of dainty white cilantro flowers to be abuzz with pollinators, especially smaller ones such as native bees and syrphid flies.

CULTIVATION Cilantro is native to Asia and Europe and grows best in cooler weather. The best time to plant cilantro is after the last frost, but while the weather is still cool. Choose a location that will get full sun. In hot weather, the cilantro plant grows quickly. To prevent bolting, which happens fast, keep the plant watered, provide afternoon shade, and regularly harvest some leaves. In warmer areas, there are varieties that are slower to bolt, such as 'Long Standing', 'Jantar', and 'Leisure'.

Dandelion

BOTANICAL OVERVIEW
Latin name: *Taraxacum officinale*
Plant family: Asteraceae

IDENTIFICATION Dandelions can be recognized by their yellow flowers and toothed leaves, and they have hollow stems. While dandelion is widely known and naturally found in most untreated lawns, there is a less common look-alike called cat's ear or false dandelion (*Hypochaeris radicata*), which has solid stems and hairier, more deeply lobed leaves.

FOOD AND NUTRITION Dandelion is a forager's friend. The leaves are delicious in the spring, and the sunny flowers can be eaten at any time. The roots are best enjoyed when they are harvested in the spring or fall.

Ways to enjoy the dandelion include:

- Leaves—raw in a green salad, sautéed as you would any other dark leafy green, or used as part of a spring pesto.
- Flowers—fried into a fritter, steeped as a fresh tea, the petals mixed into baked goods, soaked in a vinegar then used in salad dressing, or fermented into beer or wine.
- Roots—stir-fried, added to soups, cooked with potatoes, or roasted into a coffee alternative.

The dandelion plant is high in iron, manganese, phosphorus, protein, sodium, and vitamin A in the form of carotenes. The roots are also an excellent source of inulin, a water-soluble fiber that has a prebiotic effect.

ECOLOGICAL ROLE Dandelion flowers are an important source of food for pollinators such as bees, beetles, and butterflies. Some bird species eat the seeds, and the leaves are eaten by many animals, which means they might not be as likely to eat things you purposely planted. Dandelions grow and even thrive in compacted soil, and their presence helps to address this issue by creating more passageways for air and water to travel down into the soil. Soils with a large dandelion presence indicate a more bacterial, rather than fungal, soil environment.

CULTIVATION Most people won't need to cultivate dandelions, because they naturally appear seemingly everywhere. However, those who want to welcome dandelions into their edible landscape can directly sow seeds in early spring or late autumn. Dandelions are highly resilient and grow in many climates and conditions. However, they are happiest in soil with good fertility and prefer adequate moisture and ample sun.

Goji Berries

BOTANICAL OVERVIEW

Latin name: *Lycium barbarum*
Common names: Goji berry, wolfberry, boxthorn, matrimony vine
Plant family: Solanaceae

IDENTIFICATION The most distinctive feature of the goji berry plant is the fleshy bright-red fruits for which it is named. The plant has long been used for medicinal purposes, and it also can be used to create a beautiful garden hedge. A deciduous evergreen, the goji berry shrub has small, grayish-green, narrow simple leaves with an alternate arrangement and varying shapes. The small, funnel-shaped flowers have five petals and are white or bright purple and can be seen from late spring to early summer.

FOOD AND NUTRITION Goji berries are known for having a sweet, slightly sour flavor. Believed to support eye, liver, kidney, and lung health and to reduce signs of aging, they have long been a popular part of traditional medicine in Asia.

Increasingly popular as a "super food," because of their high vitamin and mineral content (especially vitamins A and C and iron), these berries are often featured in health supplements in dried, powdered, and juiced forms. You can use dried goji berries as you would other dried fruits in trail mix, granola, cereal, yogurt, and baked goods. If you rehydrate them briefly in water, they go nicely in salsas, soups, stir-fries, and smoothies. The powder and juice can be mixed into a wide range of drinks.

ECOLOGICAL ROLE The goji berry plant is native to Asia. As a member of the Solanaceae family, its ecological needs are similar to tomatoes and other nightshades. Most of the world's commercial production of goji berries is in China, but it can be found growing in nearly all of the United States and Canada. This plant is self-fertile, so it doesn't require cross-pollination, but planting several varieties next to one another can increase fruit quality and yield.

CULTIVATION Goji berries grow on perennial shrubs that need full sun and well-draining soil in order to thrive. This thorny, drought-tolerant (once established) plant is typically pruned to stay within 3 to 6 feet (1 to 2 m), but it can grow to 12 feet (3.7 m) high if left alone. If you live in areas that get especially hot in the summer, it should be planted in an area that receives afternoon shade. Conversely, if the winters get particularly cold, it can be planted in a deep pot that you can bring in and place in a sunny window. The roots spread vigorously, which is another reason to put goji berry plants in pots. You will likely need to wait until the second year to get a strong crop of berries, and you should wait for a few weeks after the berries turn red before harvesting, or they could be bitter.

Sage

BOTANICAL OVERVIEW
Latin name: *Salvia officinalis*
Common names: Garden sage, culinary sage
Plant family: Lamiaceae

IDENTIFICATION Sage is a perennial herb that can grow up to 30 inches (76 cm) tall. It is characterized by grayish-green leaves, small purple flowers, and woody stems. Its leaves are soft and aromatic, with the smell often described as woody, herbaceous, and bright. Like other members of the mint family, sage has square stems and opposite leaves.

FOOD AND NUTRITION Sage is commonly used for both culinary and medicinal purposes. This herb is extremely versatile, elevating a wide variety of dishes. It is most commonly dried and then ground up. You can dry sage by hanging it in a sunny space and leaving it for several days, or by placing it in the oven on low heat. For a more subdued taste, frying sage in a pan will mellow out the flavor. Sage can be added to oils, baked goods, meat marinades, and sauces. It can also be sprinkled over a dish or added as a garnish. Fresh sage leaves are commonly added to cocktails and other drinks for an herbal touch. Medicinally, sage can promote digestion, relieve pain and inflammation, improve memory, lower cholesterol, and much more! It is full of vitamin K, magnesium, zinc, and copper. Sage leaves are used for medicinal teas, essential oils, creams, and sprays.

ECOLOGICAL ROLE Sage is native to the Mediterranean region and is one of the oldest and most important medicinal plants documented throughout history. The earliest records of its use date back 4,000 years and show the Egyptian empire using it as a remedy for infertility. It has also been cultivated in Europe for centuries, both for culinary and medicinal purposes. In addition, sage has several ecological benefits. It is a great companion plant for brassicas, as it repels the cabbage moths, loopers, maggots, and worms that like to target that family. It also attracts bees, butterflies, and hover flies, making it perfect for increasing pollinator presence.

CULTIVATION Sage requires 6 to 8 hours of sun; it can tolerate as little as 2 hours but will not grow as well. It should be planted in a well-draining area, as saturated soil can lead to disease or attract pests. The easiest way to grow sage is to transplant it, but it can also be grown from seed once temperatures reach 65°F to 70°F (18°C to 21°C). Once fully grown, sage is relatively low-maintenance. As a perennial, it will remain productive for years, and it benefits from being pruned every spring.

Scarlet Runner Beans

BOTANICAL OVERVIEW

Latin name: *Phaseolus coccineus*

Common names: Multiflora bean, runner bean, red giant

Plant family: Fabaceae

IDENTIFICATION Scarlet runner beans are a vigorous vining plant that can grow up to 20 feet (6 m) in one season, although they grow 6 to 8 feet (1.8 to 2.4 m) in a typical garden. They are often grown as ornamental plants due to their beautiful flowers but are a great edible addition to any landscape. They appear similar to pole beans, with emerald, heart-shaped leaves that have veiny undersides. Each plant produces vibrant red flowers that open at sunrise and close at dusk. The flowers are then followed by bean pods that can grow up to 1 foot (30 cm) long. Each pod contains 6 to 10 black with pink (or tan) speckled seeds.

FOOD AND NUTRITION The English and early American settlers began growing scarlet runner beans for food in the 1600s. The bean pods can be eaten raw, baked, boiled, steamed, or sautéed. They are tougher than other bean varieties, so slicing them before cooking is recommended. They taste best while still young—they can become mealy if left to grow for too long. The seeds can be eaten fresh—similar to lima beans—or dried. Once dried, they require a long soaking and cooking time and taste similar to chestnuts. The beans are an excellent source of protein, with 29 percent of their calories coming from protein. The plant is also high in folate and vitamin C. Its flowers are edible; they taste similar to a bean and are commonly eaten in salads or as garnishes. The thick, starchy roots can also be eaten and are common in Mesoamerican cooking.

ECOLOGICAL ROLE Scarlet runner beans are native to the mountains of Mexico and Central America, where they have been cultivated for thousands of years. They can grow at higher elevations than the common bean, making them an important crop in many mountain communities. They are also highly productive, more so than common bean varieties. They are short-lived perennials but are typically grown as annuals. Their flowers are highly attractive to hummingbirds and bees, so they are a great way to promote pollinator presence.

CULTIVATION Scarlet runner beans grow best in full sunlight and rich, nutrient-dense soil. They are more cold-tolerant than other varieties but cannot withstand frosts. They should be planted after soil temperatures reach 50°F (10°C). When the plant begins flowering and growing pods, provide abundant water; mulching will help preserve soil moisture. The plants do not need to be fertilized heavily, as this will promote lush foliage instead of beans. Due to its prolific vining nature, it is best to support the plant with trellises, teepees, netting, or string. Young transplants and seedlings also need to be supported. The plants are especially vulnerable to rabbits and slugs.

Summer Squash

BOTANICAL OVERVIEW
Latin name: *Cucurbita pepo*
Common names: Many different kinds—zucchini, pattypan, crookneck pumpkins, etc.
Plant family: Cucurbitacea

IDENTIFICATION There are more than 100 varieties of squash, all of which are herbaceous annuals that are grouped into two primary categories—summer squash and winter squash. Summer squash plants are upright and spreading (around 2 feet [60 cm]). The quick-growing fruits come in a range of shapes, surfaces, and colors. The fruits need to be harvested and used quickly after they ripen, or the rinds, which are usually edible, will harden. Popular varieties of summer squash include zucchini, globe, pattypan, and crookneck.

FOOD AND NUTRITION The fruit of squash is typically cooked before it is eaten, and the seeds and flowers can also be enjoyed as a food source. Squash can be baked, roasted, steamed, sautéed, and grilled. It can be added to soups, salads, pastas, sauces, and baked goods, making it one of the most versatile foods for eating. Squash are high in fiber and antioxidants (especially beta-carotene and vitamin C), a good source of vitamin A and B, and full of minerals such as manganese, magnesium, and potassium. The nutritional properties of squash help fend off chronic diseases such as type two diabetes, heart disease, and some cancers, and they help support eye and skin health.

ECOLOGICAL ROLE Squash are native to the Americas, where they have been cultivated by indigenous peoples for at least 8,000 years, making them one of the first domesticated food crops. There are about 20 species of wild squash across North and South America, in both temperate and tropical areas. Whether wild or cultivated, squash plants are pollinated by bees—especially squash bees—and the blossoms are enjoyed by a range of pollinators, making them a lovely addition to the ecosystem. Squash do well in a variety of companion-planting scenarios, such as being supported by tall, sturdy plants and offering coverage of soil to help keep weeds away.

CULTIVATION Both summer and winter squash are some of the easiest and most abundant foods to grow. Plant your squash where they will have full sun and well-drained, nutrient-rich soil that has ideally been prepared with several inches (5 to 7 cm) of compost. Both summer and winter squash get quite big, so the plants should be spaced at least 3 to 6 feet (1 to 2 m) apart—follow the directions for the specific varieties you have selected. Squash need a lot of nutrition to bring out their best fruit, so they will benefit from feeding throughout their growing season. Pests such as squash bugs, vine borers, and cucumber beetles like to eat squash plants. If this is an issue for your plants early in their growing season, you can use net covers to protect them, but the nets will have to be removed when the plants start to bloom so they can be pollinated.

Walking Onions

BOTANICAL OVERVIEW

Latin name: *Allium* x *proliferum*
Common names: Egyptian onion, tree onion, topsetting onion
Plant family: Amaryllidaceae

IDENTIFICATION The Egyptian walking onion is a fun twist on the traditional onion. Instead of flowers, this plant produces topsets—a cluster of small onion bulblets that grow at the top of the stalk. As the topsets grow, they weigh down the stalks and cause them to fold over onto the ground. The bulblets will then root and replant themselves; they appear to "walk" across a garden, which has earned them their name. The young bulbs are green to white, and as they mature they take on a brown color. The plant will also produce some small flowers.

FOOD AND NUTRITION A member of the amaryllis plant family, walking onions are primarily grown as a perennial. All parts are edible, and the plant itself is very versatile. Overall, it tastes similar to a shallot, although the underdeveloped onions at the bottom of the plant have a spicier taste. The bulblets can be eaten raw or cooked. They are commonly pickled, sautéed, or sliced into salads. They are also great additions to vegetable and grain dishes, or they can be fried as a side dish. The smaller onion shoots, stalks, and leaves can be eaten like chives. They are commonly used in stews, stir-fries, omelets, or as a finishing herb. The flowers are also edible and can be crumbled over a dish for added flavor. The bulb of the parent plant is tough-skinned and pungent, so it is less commonly eaten. Nutritionally, walking onions are rich in thiamin, vitamin B_6, folate, magnesium, phosphorus, and zinc. The stalks are also rich in vitamin A.

ECOLOGICAL ROLE This perennial plant is a hybrid of the Welsh onion. It was originally brought from the Indian subcontinent by migrant settlers looking to bring hardy, familiar onions to their new home. The plant gained popularity in Europe, and it was brought from Europe to the United States around 1850. They produce more bulblets than other alliums and can form additional stems above existing bulblets to form a second layer of bulblets. Thus, they have a higher yield than many other types of onions, making them beneficial for people with smaller gardens. Walking onions make great companion plants for a variety of fruits and vegetables. They can be planted with fruit trees and bushes to help combat pests, and they are one of few plants that can grow in proximity to walnut trees.

CULTIVATION Walking onions are hardy in planting zones 3–9. They prefer full sun and will be most productive when they receive six hours a day, although they can be grown in partial shade. They thrive in nutrient-rich soil and benefit from compost and other organic matter. They can tolerate weeds and various soil compositions. They are susceptible to fungal diseases like powdery mildew and black spot. To prevent these, ensure that plants have good air circulation and are not overwatered. Consider also mulching underneath to prevent pathogen transmission. Walking onions are extremely easy to propagate; simply break off the bulblets and plant them in the ground.

6

GARDEN PLANS AND MENUS

An edible landscape blends formal vegetable gardens with growing vegetables, fruits, herbs, and culinary flowers in non-traditional spaces. It really is just a matter of looking at spaces differently and having a general plan to fill those spaces with both old and new edible plant varieties. Finding new food crops is as much fun as finding offbeat places for standard crops. You may even want to include flowers for cutting or other non-food plants that support wildlife and pollinators. The main concern with adding these plants is how wide and tall they will get when mature, so you can plant them in a way that doesn't impact the growth of the food crops.

Left: While it's easy to spot the kale, chard, and peppers, it's much more challenging to see the other edible plants in this garden, including hostas, violas, violets, roses, and a hops vine.

This collection of edible "weeds" includes some great plants that are easy to find in most backyards or public parks, including sorrel, dead nettle, lamb's quarters, wood sorrel, chickweed, and more.

Edible nasturtium plants mingle with chard and the edible blossoms of an oregano plant.

Your unique planting plan will depend on the variables we already discussed in this book. It is important to have fun creating your space and learn as you grow. We want to present you with plant options and themes that we use in our gardens, not a rigid set of instructions that might constrain you. The planting menus found in this chapter contain a mix of food plants. Select the plants that are of most interest to you, and don't feel you must replicate the entire menu exactly.

The main things to keep in mind when planting your beds are the amount of sunlight, the ease of watering and caring for each bed, and the shade cast by plants when the bed has matured. Approach these menus with the idea that you can either randomly scatter seeds and tuck in plants where there is open space, or you can more formally plant them in rows and patterns. It is about what you like to see when walking through your gardens. The creative options are really endless.

Right: Blackberries are a must-have fruiting cane in Gary's garden.

EDIBLE FLOWER GARDEN

A great way to expand your edible landscaping journey is with edible flowers. They offer so much beauty to your landscape, and they are discreet. If you have any concerns about your neighbors or home-owners' association taking issue with you growing food, they might not even know what you are up to.

The following is a list of edible flowers that can be used as stand-alone edible landscape elements or used to surround other food crops. Most of these plants are well-loved by a diverse range of pollinators, so you can use these edibles to create a gorgeous pollinator garden somewhere front and center in your landscape.

EDIBLE FLOWER GARDEN MENU

Plant	Planting Tips	How to Eat and Enjoy
Bee Balm *Monarda fistulosa*	Plant in full sun. Though it can tolerate some shade, it can get leggy. It is related to mint and will spread aggressively.	Leaves and flowers can be used. It has a minty oregano taste. It can be used in teas.
Calendula *Calendula officinalis*	Prefers a cool climate and tolerates frost well. Plant seeds in partial shade to full sun in well-drained soil.	Beautiful tangy orange flowers can be used to color rice and other dishes. Makes a great salad garnish.
Daylily *Hemerocallis fulva*	They prefer full sun but can still bloom well with 4–6 hours of sun. They like almost any soil and are very hardy.	The flowers are edible and delicious raw, in salads, or very lightly sautéed.
Hollyhock *Alcea rosea*	Plant in full sun in a place that is protected from the wind. Remove seed heads so that you can enjoy blooms year after year.	The leaves, petals, and roots can be used in teas. Hollyhocks have a light, slightly bitter, vegetable flavor.
Hyssop *Hyssopus officinalis*	Easy and versatile to grow! Plant it in light shade to full sun in either dry or moist, well-drained soil.	Mint-flavored flowers can be pickled, preserved, and added to soups, sauces, and casseroles. Don't eat if you are pregnant or have had seizures.
Common Lilac *Syringa vulgaris*	They are best planted in the fall as the season is ending but can be planted in early spring when freeze has passed. They prefer full sun.	The flowers are edible and best used steeped in syrup or used in teas. They can be eaten raw. They can even be soaked in cream to infuse it.
Mallow *Malva sylvestris*	They prefer partial shade or sun and like drier soil. They need at least 3 feet (1 m) of space. They can manage well in low-water areas. They are very easy to grow.	The leaves and flowers can be used in salads. Even the roots can be used in teas.
Pansy *Viola x wittrockiana*	Plant in partial shade to full sun in well-drained soil rich in organic matter.	The entire pansy flower can be eaten and has a mild wintergreen-flavored flower that makes a candied garnish.
Primrose *Primula vulgaris*	Plant this perennial in shady to partially sunny woodland conditions with moist soil, even clay.	The leaves and flowers have a mild to tangy flavor for salads, soups, syrups, and teas. The flower buds can be pickled or fermented for wine.
Scented Geraniums *Pelargonium* spp.	Plant in full sun (partial shade in hotter climates) in well-drained soil. Overwinter indoors and pinch back spent blossoms.	The leaves and flowers can be used to flavor teas, sugars, syrups, oils, or other infusions. They can also be added into baked goods.

Hyssop

Bee Balm

Primrose

Calendula

Daylily

Mallow

Scented Geraniums

Hollyhock

Lilac

An edible flower garden field is ready for harvest. Included are borage, calendula, chamomile, and others.

You can even grow herbs vertically by planting them in wall-mounted pockets of soil to create a living wall.

Even if you only have room for a few containers, herbs make a wonderful choice.

CULINARY HERB GARDEN

Herbs are some of the easiest plants to grow. They are a great addition to any edible landscape and can be successfully grown in any space with more sun than not. Having fresh herbs available when cooking helps to make meals more delicious, healthy, and fragrant. Your herbs can be planted as seeds or transplants and do equally well in containers or the ground.

CULINARY HERB GARDEN MENU

Plant	Planting Tips	How to Eat and Enjoy
Basil *Ocimum basilicum*	Prefers warm weather and is best planted by seed every 3 weeks to ensure continued crops of tender leaves.	Leaves can be used fresh or dried. Basil is used primarily to make pesto.
Chives *Allium schoenoprasum*	A perennial in most gardens and very hard to kill. The flowers are best used just after bloom.	Leaves can be used fresh or dried. Flowers can be used in salads.
Cilantro *Coriandrum sativum*	Enjoys cooler weather but can be planted through the summer. The mature seeds, called coriander, can be harvested and used in cooking.	Leaves are best used fresh. It is a wonderful addition to salsas. The seeds can be harvested after they dry on the plant.
Dill *Anethum graveolens*	A warm-weather crop that is best planted by seed every few weeks. Many butterflies and pollinators enjoy dill flowers.	Leaves can be used fresh. It is excellent as a pickling spice and with yogurt or sour cream to make dips.
Oregano *Origanum vulgare*	A perennial plant that makes a great ground-cover and can be planted almost anywhere. They don't like to grow in consistently wet soil.	Leaves can be used fresh or dried.
Parsley *Petroselinum crispum*	Parsley can be a slow germinator and is best planted as a transplant. It is also enjoyed as a food by many butterflies.	Leaves can be used fresh or dried.
Rosemary *Salvia rosmarinus*	A perennial in many areas if temperature infrequently drops below 20°F (-7°C).	Leaves are best used fresh.
Sage *Salvia officinalis*	A perennial that can take a beating. It is best managed by cutting old dead and lanky growth off in the spring.	Leaves are best used fresh.
Thyme *Thymus vulgaris*	Thyme is a wonderful perennial groundcover. The new growth is best for cooking. Old growth should be cut back in early spring.	Leaves can be used fresh or dried.

TEA GARDEN

If you enjoy tea, there are many plants you can grow so you can brew your own cup straight from the garden. You can have a dedicated tea garden, incorporate these plants throughout your edible landscape, or use containers to highlight your favorite plants for tea brewing. Most tea-garden plants prefer substantial sunlight and loamy, well-draining soil with a pH between 5 and 7. You can use most of these plants fresh or dry for making tea. For a fresh tea, grab the flowers or leaves you want, rinse them, place them in a cup with boiling water, and steep for five to ten minutes, adding sweetener to taste.

TEA GARDEN MENU

Plant	Planting Tips	How to Eat and Enjoy
Borage *Borago officinalis*	An easy-to-grow annual. Plant in partial to full sun in a place protected from the wind. Borage prefers soil that is loose and drains well. It can be sown by seed after the last frost.	The leaves and flowers are both edible but should be used fresh and sparingly. The leaves can be enjoyed raw, sautéed, or candied. The bright-blue flowers, which have a cucumber taste, attract pollinators and brighten up a salad.
Chamomile *Matricaria chamomilla*	Easy to start indoors for transplants and easily grown by direct seeding. It is not a perennial but reseeds like crazy. Direct seeding is done a few weeks before the last frost.	Flowers flavor jams, ice cream, liquor, just about anything you can think of. Its flowers are commonly used for making teas to be sipped before bedtime.
Echinacea *Echinacea purpurea*	A hardy and common perennial in many areas. It can be propagated by division or started as seeds in the spring. It tolerates many conditions.	Flowers and leaves are edible but they are best used in teas. They don't add much when eaten raw.
Ginger *Zingiber officinale*	Prefers 4–6 hours of sun and does not like full sun. It can take 8–10 months to fully mature, so starting ginger indoors is a good idea. It should be planted when frost has well passed.	Ginger root is used in so many ways: candied, pressed, chopped, in teas, etc. It is a plant that would grow well in the shade of other plants.
Jasmine *Jasminum sambac*	Can tolerate partial shade but flowers best in full sun. It prefers well-draining soil that stays moist but not soaking wet. It can do well in pots.	Jasmine flowers are best mixed with your favorite dried teas to add flavor. Or the flowers can be used directly with hot water.
Lavender *Lavandula angustifolia*	Prefers maximum sun and well-draining soil. Doesn't like wet roots. Do not over-water. Best planted as transplants. Seeds can take a long time to germinate, and they grow slowly. Different varieties may be better suited for your winters.	Simply steep a bunch of fresh flowers for 10 minutes in hot water for a delicious fragrant tea.
Lemon Balm *Melissa officinalis*	Lemon balm is very easy to grow from seeds or transplants. The leaves are full of lemon scent and flavor. Does well with 6 or more hours of sun. Makes a great container plant.	Simply crush the leaves in your hand and release the oils and aroma. The leaves can be steeped in hot water.
Lemon Verbena *Aloysia citriodora*	Lemon verbena may be a perennial if your area has mild winters. It is best grown as a transplant, and it does really well in containers. It prefers full sun.	The leaves are used like lemon balm.
Mint *Mentha* spp.	Does well in full sun and partial shade. It is aggressive and will take over a yard. It is best grown in containers. If grown in the ground, it needs to be tended well. It is a hardy perennial in most gardens.	Mint, spearmint, and peppermint leaves make wonderful teas, fresh or dried.

If you dry your tea plants so they are available throughout the year, remember that drying increases the intensity of the flavor. With any new plant, make sure you buy the variety that is grown for consumption.

Right: This box of dried plants shows the diversity of plants that can be used to make teas, including rose hips, clover, chamomile, bachelor's buttons, and more.

Borage

Chamomile

Echinacea

Jasmine

Potatoes, fava beans, and the soft, feathery leaves of fennel make a beautiful anchor for an edible landscape.

Bowls full of greens can be harvested regularly from plants tucked throughout a landscape.

EDIBLE GREENS

Here is a list of edible greens that can be tucked all over the landscape. Most of them prefer cooler soil and temperatures, as they tend to bolt and flower when the heat of summer arrives. In many places they can be planted in the spring and again in the fall. Enjoy them raw or cooked. When harvesting, we recommend taking a couple of leaves or cutting off the mature leaves as a bunch at soil level. If you leave the roots in, more leaves will come. A trick for the heat of summer is to plant them next to taller plants that cast shade and will keep them cool.

EDIBLE GREENS MENU

Plant	Planting Tips	How to Eat and Enjoy
Lettuce *Lactuca sativa*	Lettuces can be planted closely together for harvest as baby greens or 4–6 inches (10–15 cm) apart for larger heads.	Leaves are perfect for salads, and sturdy lettuce variety leaves make great wraps.
Spinach *Spinacia oleracea*	Can be planted just like lettuce. They are very frost tolerant and can handle fall frosts well.	Leaves used in salads or cooked down.
Arugula *Eruca vesicaria*	Fast-growing with a peppery, nutty flavor. Arugula can be planted like lettuce.	Raw in salads or added as late additions to sautées or scrambled eggs.
Endive *Cichorium endivia*	A firmer leaf with a pleasant amount of bitterness. They do best with a space of at least 4 inches (10 cm).	Cut as a head, they are wonderful as the main leaves in a salad. The sturdier leaves hold a dressing nicely.
Mustard Greens *Brassica juncea*	Mustard greens can get quite large and need at least 6 inches (15 cm) of space. They have a spicy mustard taste when raw, especially when the days get hotter.	Sautéeing them greatly reduces the spiciness and mustard flavor of the leaves.
Turnip Greens *Brassica rapa var. rapa*	A hardy green for those beds that might be neglected. They are fast growers that enjoy cool temperatures.	Added to salad or sautéed with butter.
Kale *Brassica oleracea*	Does well in cool and warm weather. They taste sweeter in cool temperatures. They will get large and do best with 6–12 inches (15–30 cm) of space.	Delicious raw in salads or cooked down with onion. The buds and flowers are edible and make delicious additions to salads and scrambled eggs.
Collards *Brassica oleracea*	Treat them like kale. They do tend to flower and bolt faster than kale.	They can be used like kale.
Bunching Onions *Allium fistulosum*	They will grow through the spring, summer, and fall in most areas. They are best planted scattered within 1 inch (2.5 cm) of each other in long lines.	The greens can be chopped and used raw or cooked. The lower part of the stem has a strong onion flavor, while the upper green stem is quite mild.

SALAD TRIMMINGS

While leafy greens make the base of a salad, the following plants make wonderful trimmings for all kinds of dishes. Some of these can be planted close to the leafy greens. A small handful of plants pulled from this garden will bring crunch and color to the plate. Edible flowers will bring their own flavor and sophistication to any dish.

SALAD TRIMMINGS MENU

Plant	Planting Tips	How to Eat and Enjoy
Radish *Raphanus raphanistrum* subsp. *sativus*	Radishes prefer cool weather, and seeds can be scattered and raked into the soil surface. Plant about 50 seeds at a time every 2 weeks.	Most radishes can be harvested 25–40 days after germination. The young greens can be used in salads. The matured greens can be sautéed as they get a bit prickly.
Bunching Onions *Allium fistulosum*	See **Edible Greens Menu**, page 143, for details.	See **Edible Greens Menu**, page 143, for details.
Carrots *Daucus carota* subsp. *sativus*	Carrots are best planted by seed in the early spring and can take many weeks to germinate. We recommend short varieties of carrots as they do better in compacted soil.	Carrots can be eaten raw or baked with some brown sugar and butter. The greens can be sautéed or made into pesto.
Garlic *Allium sativum*	Garlic cloves can be planted 1–3 inches (2.5–7.5 cm) deep based on how cold your winters get. Hardneck garlic should be planted in the fall and softneck garlic can be planted in early spring.	Garlic bulbs may not fully form at times, but you will get something delicious to use every time. The greens are outstanding raw and cooked.
Pansy *Viola x wittrockiana*	Plant in partial shade to full sun in an area that doesn't stay overly wet. Pansies are best planted as transplants.	The entire pansy flower can be eaten. The mild wintergreen-flavored flower makes a nice candied garnish. Add flowers after a salad is dressed.
Common Blue Violet *Viola sororia*	Plant in partial shade to full sun. Violets are best planted as transplants. Plant them in the sun when it is cooler and in shady areas as the summer arrives.	The entire flower is edible. Drop the flower heads in water to help crisp them up before dropping them in a salad. Add flowers after the salad is dressed.
Nasturtium *Tropaeolum majus*	Plant seeds when the soil warms and the chance for frost has passed. Remove flowers regularly to encourage more blooms and discourage seed formation.	All parts of the plant are edible, including immature seed pods. Nasturtiums have a mild peppery bite that strengthens as the days get warmer. The plant is best used raw.

Pansy

Edible Chive and Kale Flowers

Nasturtium

Don't focus solely on ground beds. Leafy greens
and other food crops do well in vertical towers too.

A mix of popular root crops freshly harvested from Gary's garden.

HARDY ROOT CROPS

These are some of the more hardy root crops that can do well in beds that might be more difficult to tend or need time for the soil to improve in quality. Garlic is planted from cloves and horseradish should be planted from a sprouted piece of root. The rest are best planted by seed. These plants can be planted early when it is cool and frost is still a risk.

Right: Community Ecology Institute (CEI) team member Justin Chen harvesting radishes at Freetown Farm.

HARDY ROOT CROPS MENU

Plant	Planting Tips	How to Eat and Enjoy
Beets *Beta vulgaris*	Beets should be planted with 4 inches (10 cm) between them.	They can be grown for harvesting the greens or for mature beets. Roasted beets are delicious.
Turnips *Brassica rapa* var. *rapa*	Turnips can be planted like beets. They are a faster-maturing root crop and should be planted in waves every 2–3 weeks.	They can be grown for immature greens for salads. The mature leaves can be sautéed. Mature turnips can be roasted or mashed like potatoes.
Radishes *Raphanus raphanistrum* subsp. *sativus*	See **Salad Trimmings Menu**, page 144, for details.	See **Salad Trimmings Menu**, page 144, for details.
Onions *Allium cepa*	Onions are very frost tolerant and should be planted by seed as soon as the soil can be worked. A general spacing of a few inches (5–7 cm) is best.	The onion bulbs and greens can be eaten.
Garlic *Allium sativum*	See **Salad Trimmings Menu**, page 144, for details.	See **Salad Trimmings Menu**, page 144, for details.
Rutabaga *Brassica napus*	The bulb can get to the size of a softball. They should be planted with at least 6 inches (15 cm) between them.	The greens can be sautéed. Although the root can get quite large, they taste best when picked at 3–5 inches (7.5–12.5 cm).
Horseradish *Armoracia rusticana*	Horseradish loves cooler soil and can use some summer shade. It is very easy to grow as a transplant. Once established it keeps growing and expanding.	Harvest pieces of the root as you need them during the summer and fall. They are perfect for bringing heat to sauces.

A mix of cool- and warm-loving food crops ensures harvests through the seasons. These cold-tolerant radishes were pulled from the garden after the season's first snowfall.

Blueberries can replace many non-edible shrubs because they are beautiful all season long.

A handful of fruits is a common occurrence in Gary's edible landscape as berries are everywhere!

Muscadines and green beans create a living tunnel thanks to the support of a cattle panel trellis.

FRUIT AND BERRY PATCH

If you enjoy handfuls of fresh-picked fruit, a berry patch is for you. Check the spacing needs of each plant and remember to plant with a plan to ensure the mature plants won't impact the surrounding plants. It is also important to check if the plants you select can manage the winters in your garden. There is nothing sweeter than the sugars from fresh-picked fruits and berries.

FRUIT AND BERRY PATCH MENU

Plant	Planting Tips	How to Eat and Enjoy
Blueberries *Vaccinium* sect. *Cyanococcus*	Plant two different varieties to maximize pollination and berry plumpness. They prefer to have damp roots through the heat of the summer.	Mix varieties as there are early, mid-, and late-maturing varieties. Harvest handfuls when dark, plump, and sweet.
Blackberries *Rubus* subg. *Rubus*	Blackberries are spectacular fruit canes that can get 10 feet (3 m) tall. Clumping varieties of blackberries are available for small spaces and even larger containers.	When the blackberry turns a deep purple and their glossy shine begins to dull, they are ready to harvest.
Currants *Ribes* spp.	Currants come in black, red, and white varieties. They prefer full sun but can manage with partial shade. They have shallow roots that need to be watered regularly in the summer. They do well in containers.	They ripen in June and July over a several-week period. Keep an eye on them. Pick when plump, colorful, and soft to the touch.
Goji Berries *Lycium barbarum*	Goji berries prefer full sun and can manage drought. They are very susceptible to rotting roots if the soil is a heavy clay that stays wet. They should be pruned to manage the size and height of the plant.	Goji berries are ready to be harvested when they look plump and are a brilliant orange red, which is about 4–5 weeks after flowers have bloomed. They are not overly sweet and can be enjoyed in salads or mixed with rice or side dishes.
Gooseberries *Ribes* spp.	Gooseberries are self-pollinating. They prefer sunny areas and well-drained soil. They have thorns and should be well pruned to manage the plant.	Gooseberries ripen late June through mid-July. They will be soft when ready to pick. The longer they stay on the vine, the sweeter they get. They are perfect for jams and pies.
Lingonberries *Vaccinium vitis-idaea*	They need to have a pollinator for maximum yield and berry size. Two varieties are required. They prefer the sun and like heat and dry roots.	They have two harvest times in spring and later summer. They are more acidic and should be picked when firm and red in color. With a similar taste to a cranberry, they are best cooked.
Muscadine Grapes *Vitis rotundifolia*	They grow very similarly to grapes but are more prolific and need heavier dormant pruning to manage vine size and maintain regular fruiting. They are best grown on a fence or trellis.	They produce a firm berry that is tart and sweet. Allow it to stay on the vine longer than you might want to for more sweetness. The skin should indent lightly when pressed.
Raspberries *Rubus* spp.	Raspberries come in various colors and growth habits. They can be invasive and are best grown as clumping varieties. They prefer full sun but can manage in partial shade. Trellising is recommended.	Raspberries are delicious fresh-picked when soft and easily pulled from the cane. They are absolutely one of the best hand-to-mouth berries around.
Strawberries *Fragaria* x *ananassa*	Can be planted all around the base of your berry patch. They make a wonderful groundcover. They will help manage moisture in the planting area. Freshly harvested and seasonally shipped bare roots are the best way to plant them.	Harvest strawberries when fully red and soft to the touch. They can be enjoyed fresh or sliced with honey.

PERENNIAL VEGETABLES

Many of the above plants are perennials, especially the herbs and fruits and berries, but here is a menu of vegetables that are perennials in many gardens. It is always important to research the hardiness of each crop and match it to your seasonal temperatures. A perennial vegetable garden can take time to get started, but once it is established, it produces year after year.

An edible landscape should be a thing of beauty, with a great diversity of productive plants, including many perennials.

Artichoke

Asparagus

Lovage

Rhubarb

PERENNIAL VEGETABLES MENU

Plant	Planting Tips	How to Eat and Enjoy
Artichoke *Cynara cardunculus var. scolymus*	They get tall and are best planted where they won't overshadow other plants. They are perennials where winters are mild. Mulching will add winter protection to their roots. They prefer full sun.	Petal bases, stem center, and heart or center of the bud are edible. Typically cooked with butter until soft.
Asparagus *Asparagus officinalis*	After spring harvests, asparagus needs to be left to grow, and it can reach heights of 5 feet (1.5 m). Plant with a strategy for its shade to fall outside the bed.	Harvest early in the season. The immature stems can be eaten raw, sautéed, or chopped up and cooked with rice. A great way to prepare them is a quick broil.
Cardoons *Cynara cardunculus*	Similar growth habits as artichokes. Space needs will vary based on how you harvest the plants.	Stems are picked and often blanched. They can be eaten raw like celery.
Groundnut (Peanut) *Arachis hypogaea*	They prefer loose well-draining soil and full sun. They grow about 18 inches (45 cm) tall. Groundnuts take 150 days to mature.	Groundnuts can be roasted or used raw.
Lovage *Levisticum officinale*	It can get to be 5 feet (1.5 m). Like any tall crop, plant at the back or side of your garden space. It grows easily from seed and prefers full sun.	Leaves are wonderful in salads or as late additions to soup. It can be used to make vegetable stock. Tastes very similar to celery.
Rhubarb *Rheum rhabarbarum*	Rhubarb does not like hot afternoon sun or wet roots. Plant it where it gets shade from taller plants. It is best planted as divisions or transplants.	Leaves are not eaten and are toxic. The stems are used and are quite tart. They are most often used for pies or cooked dishes.
Sorrel *Rumex acetosa*	Grows very easily from seed. Plant seeds 3 weeks before the last frost. Once a plant is established, it can be divided yearly for new plants. It grows to a height of 18 inches (45 cm) tall.	Leaves have a tangy, citrusy, tart flavor. It is used mixed with salad greens or is steamed or sautéed.
Walking Onions *Allium x proliferum*	A perennial plant that flops over and slowly walks across your garden. They are planted from bulbils that form on the tip of the plant. They prefer full sun but can manage in partial shade. They grow to the height of standard onions.	The bulblets on the tips of the stems are eaten raw, cooked, or pickled. Young stems can be used like chives.

Use these menus to select plants for your earth beds or containers, or tuck some of them into your existing beds. As mentioned, keep plant height in mind and how shade falls from them. Use the shade of the taller edibles for plants that dislike afternoon sun. Plant with a general plan and enjoy your gardens. Next, let's discuss how to plant and care for your edible landscape.

7

PLANTING AND TENDING YOUR GARDENS

Gary's edible landscape contains a large garden of fruits and vegetables, two smaller gardens of mixed edibles, a small orchard, and several areas with combinations of trees, bushes, flowers, and edible plants. The food-producing plants throughout his landscape are a mix of traditional vegetables, dwarf fruit trees, blueberry bushes, strawberry plants, fruiting canes, herbs, and nontraditional edible plants. No matter what we are growing across our property, our plants will need to be planted and tended. This chapter provides an introduction to the tools you'll need to successfully plant and tend your edible landscape.

Left: Properly planting and tending your edible landscape is essential for success.

A sunny backyard garden filled with edibles is easier to care for because it's close to the house, rather than being in a far-away corner of the yard.

PLANT NUTRIENTS AND FERTILIZERS

Your plants need six main elements for healthy productive growth, as well as other micronutrients and trace minerals. The main three elements that are consumed at higher levels are called primary macronutrients, and they are nitrogen, phosphorus, and potassium. Nitrogen in particular is used heavily by plants and often needs to be replenished yearly in garden beds. The other three elements, called secondary macronutrients, are sulfur, magnesium, and calcium. They too must be present in the soil but are consumed in lower quantities. In short, we have to feed our growing areas regularly to replace the soil nutrients used by our plants as they grow.

Plants can be fed through the use of fertilizers, animal manures, and compost. Fertilizers typically come in slow-release and fast-release forms. They focus on providing the six main elements to plants but don't necessarily feed and support soil life or help in building healthy soil structure. That will be addressed when we discuss compost in a later section.

What Do the Numbers Mean on a Fertilizer Package?

Any packaged fertilizer you buy will have three numbers on it. They represent the primary macronutrients your plants need in the order of nitrogen (N), phosphorus (P), and potassium (K), or NPK. A 5-5-5 NPK is considered a balanced fertilizer as the bag, by weight, contains 5% nitrogen, 5% phosphorus, and 5% potassium. We recommend buying fertilizers with numbers that come close to a balance, because it is hard to find balanced organic fertilizers. The numbers vary on different packages—for example you might find a 5-3-3 NPK, a 3-5-6 NPK, or 4-2-7 NPK. To make things more confusing, the bag might say tomato fertilizer, leafy green fertilizer, heirloom fertilizer, or fruit and berry fertilizer. It is true that different percentages of nitrogen, phosphorus, and potassium can influence plant development at different growth stages. However, it really isn't something to worry about for home gardens. As you become a more experienced gardener, you can look more into feeding plants with varying ratios of N, P, and K at different growth stages if you find that interesting. Simply make sure N, P, and K are represented in the bag you buy. You don't need to pay attention to the brand name, just purchase what is most budget friendly—your plants don't care about fancy packaging and words. A bag of heirloom tomato fertilizer will take care of lettuce, peppers, beans, radishes, fruits, and berries equally well. Plants just want nitrogen, phosphorus, and potassium made available to them consistently.

ORGANIC FERTILIZERS

Organic fertilizers are wonderful for a garden and should be used instead of synthetic chemical fertilizers when possible because they provide nutrients for the plants and also help feed soil life. Organic fertilizers are typically made from the organic matter of plants and animals. It is important to look for the ingredients listed on the packaging of bagged fertilizers. Plant examples are dried seaweed, often called kelp meal, or the spent seeds from cotton seed oil extraction, often called cottonseed meal. You might also see bone meal on the fertilizer package. This is high in phosphorus and calcium and is usually derived from pulverized cattle bones. If your garden needs nitrogen, plants' most-used element, you might buy a bag of blood meal—dried bovine blood from slaughterhouses. The term "meal" is used generically to describe components of organic fertilizers.

To make organic fertilizers, many different ingredients can be blended together to change the amounts of nitrogen, phosphorus, potassium, and other elements in the packaged product. You will find many of the same basic ingredients in various bags of blended organic fertilizers, but the cost varies greatly across different brands. We recommend buying the least expensive per pound. There is no magical fertilizer, but there are plenty of overpriced products.

You will find most organic granular fertilizers cost about $2 USD per pound (0.5 kg). An alternative to this is buying 50-pound (23-kg) bags of alfalfa animal feed pellets for about $25 USD. The savings can be as much as 75% when compared to commercial bagged fertilizers. The pellets add some organic matter to the soil, provide nitrogen, phosphorus, and potassium to the plants, and have a natural plant growth hormone that benefits plant root systems. The pellets can be sprinkled in containers, around plants, and across all gardens in your edible landscape. The pellets are large and should be watered in with a hose or applied when rain is expected. The pellets expand, once wet, into flakes that easily get worked into the soil. If you are concerned about chemicals on alfalfa, you can buy organic pellets.

Gary uses alfalfa pellets for an early spring raised-bed refresh.

SLOW-RELEASE ORGANIC FERTILIZERS

Slow-release organic fertilizers come in a dry formulation, often as granules and sometimes as compressed pellets. The nitrogen, phosphorus, potassium, and other nutrients are not fully available to the plants in this form. Plants will get some minimal benefit initially, but the slow-release organic granules need to be broken down by the soil life and changed into a form the plants can absorb through their roots. This typically occurs over several months. Each week, the microbes slowly break down some of the granular fertilizer and make nutrients available to the plants. It is very similar to what happens in the composting process. This type of fertilizer is often used by mixing it thoroughly in the planting hole or by scattering it around the surface of the soil. It sets the plants up with a slow, steady release of nutrients over a prolonged period.

FAST-RELEASE ORGANIC FERTILIZERS

Fast-release organic fertilizers are typically mixed with water and provide nutrients that are immediately available to the plants through their roots. Plants are also able to absorb some nutrients through their leaves, which is known as a foliar feeding. The bottom line is the plant gets the nutrients it needs to grow almost immediately. These water-soluble fertilizers or fast-release fertilizers are often higher in nitrogen than other elements. That is because nitrogen helps with leaf growth and development. Generally speaking, any tree, bush, or plant that goes in your garden would benefit from this type of organic fertilizer when first planted. Ongoing use and frequency of application varies based on what is being grown. Organic fertilizers, both slow- and fast-release forms, benefit the plants but don't contain enough organic matter to build good soil structure and feed all the soil microbes and life, as is truly needed for a thriving garden ecosystem. Compost, on the other hand, delivers all of the benefits for a healthy soil ecosystem at all levels (see compost section that follows).

Budget Saver #5: The Fertilizer Name Game

When you first start gardening, you are going to be overwhelmed by the number of fertilizers on the market. You are misled to believe you need specialized fertilizers for everything growing in your garden. You don't. You only need one bag of granular fertilizer and one brand of water-soluble fertilizer. They can be used effectively on any plant. Then, you might ask, why are the shelves filled with products that have specific names like Flower-tone®, Heirloom Tomato Fertilizer, Bulb Boosting Fertilizer, and so many more? The answer is to get you to spend more money by buying multiple bags of their fertilizers. But plants don't care about the name, and neither should we; they just want to be fed. Buy one type of fertilizer and use it for all your flowers, fruits, vegetables, and herbs. Don't get caught up in the fertilizer name game.

Gary applying liquid fertilizer to onions.

SOIL, MANURE, AND COMPOST

Organic fertilizers provide some benefits to soil structure and soil microbes, but not enough. Soil needs a lot of organic matter year after year. The main quantity of organic matter needed for gardens should come from manures and compost, not from bagged synthetic fertilizers. Compost is fully decomposed organic matter that feeds plants, soil microbes, and earthworms, and contributes to building up the structure of the garden's soil. Compost is greatly underused. Yes, compost can be expensive to purchase, especially when compared to making your own (which we'll discuss in a moment).

The soil in our geographically different planting areas will vary. The soil may even vary across your property. Wonderful soil is the key to a thriving edible landscape of fruits, vegetables, flowers, and herbs, but it is not created at planting, in a week, or even over a year's time. Soil is built year after year, over the lifetime of the planting beds, and that is why we recommend regular use of manures and compost. As we have stressed, there is no need to feel you have to have "perfect" soil before you start planting.

Making your own compost is a money-saving way to make your own fertilizer and soil amendment. This is one of the composting areas Gary uses to maintain his edible landscape.

Synthetic Chemical Fertilizers

The distinction between organic fertilizers and synthetic chemical fertilizers depends on whether they are made through chemistry or through a naturally occurring process. Synthetic chemical fertilizers are processed by people in some form, often through mixing chemical compounds together. They are not made purely from organic materials, and they do not provide significant benefits to the structure of the soil or to the microbes living in it. They are, however, effective in providing the nutrients plants need to grow. They are not toxic to plants or poisonous to us (when used according to label instructions), but they are not as beneficial as organic fertilizers. Overuse of any type of fertilizer—synthetic chemical ones in particular—can create issues with excess nutrient runoff into waterways, which is very harmful to the environment. Gary uses synthetic products only occasionally in emergency spot treatments and sometimes in containers to help his plants grow without concern.

For plants to really thrive, it is also important to build up the structure of the soil and feed the microbes living in it. Since synthetic chemical fertilizers don't do that, organic fertilizers and compost make for better choices. Healthy soil leads to stronger and healthier plants. Take care of the soil and the soil will take care of your plants is a guideline we can't stress enough.

That belief actually becomes a barrier for many people to get started, and it can be extremely expensive to try to make "perfect" soil immediately. If you have grass, weeds, or flowers growing where you want to grow edible food, you can plant there.

The goal is to begin building and expanding your edible landscape sooner rather than later. The short version is that you can amend the planting hole for each plant to ensure it grows well. We use organic fertilizer to amend the beds and just get things started. Homemade compost will eventually feed the plants in subsequent years and build the soil over time. The key to quality compost is ensuring it is fully broken down before using it. It takes time for organic matter to fully decompose; we need to be patient and let Nature work. The requirements to start composting are fairly simple.

But before we get to building compost piles, it is important to understand that composting is the process of decomposing organic matter down into basic elements. The organic matter used to make compost may be animal-based, such as manures, or plant-based, such as leaves, grass clippings, weeds, spent garden plants, or kitchen vegetable scraps. The simplest way to look at it is to understand that the term composting really means allowing bacteria, fungi, molds, worms, and other organisms to digest and decompose organic matter and turn it into dark, nutrient-rich humus over time. Humus is the end product of natural decay. It is what forest floors are made of, and we want to copy that process in our edible landscapes by using compost. We fondly call this finished, fully decayed organic matter compost or "black gold." It is everything our plants and soil need to thrive.

A handful of beautiful compost ready for garden beds!

What Is the Biggest Mistake Made When Composting?

Compost feeds plants, soil microbes, earthworms, and other soil life, and it builds and maintains the structure of the soil as Nature intended. It is free to make, and it is fully sustainable. Compost provides all the nutrients your plants need, just like decaying organic matter on a forest floor feeds the forest. It makes for very happy and active microbes and earthworms by giving them food to eat and places to live and multiply. It provides everything needed to develop a healthy soil ecosystem. The root systems of your edible plants will flourish and thrive in soil that has been built over the years with compost. Stronger root systems support vigorous plant growth, encourage food production, and increase the ability of plants to manage attacks from pests and disease. Composting, when you have the space, should be started when you plant your first garden. Amazing soil is something you work toward year after year, but it can't begin until you have a large amount of composted organic matter. The biggest mistake people make when thinking about composting is simply not getting started. We now recommend gardeners build their first compost pen before building their first garden bed.

Gary's cold-composting bins regularly offer up their "black gold."

Cold Composting vs Hot Composting

Cold composting is a passive process that decomposes organic matter slowly over time. There is also hot composting, which requires alternating layers of greens (nitrogen-rich organic matter, such as grass clippings) with layers of browns (carbon-rich organic matter, such as leaves). This is a very active process that requires turning the piles several times a week. Hot composting increases the rate of decay of the materials in the pile. The pile actually heats up to 140°F (60°C). The heated composting process can deliver completed compost in as little as 90 days.

Cold composting is nothing more than putting organic matter into a pile and letting Nature do the work. This can take 6 months to a year, sometimes longer. However, after that first year, you will have compost available year after year, assuming you keep adding organic matter to the pile. Cold composting is what we recommend to get started. It will feed your plants and soil life, and it will help maintain the structure of your soil. Plus, it keeps yard debris out of the landfill. This is the best way to take care of your edible landscape for many years to come.

A wire dog pen provides a basic design for a compost bin.

A compost pen that opens in the front can be built quickly and easily out of posts and wire fencing.

BUILDING A COMPOST PEN

The standard dimensions for a compost pile are 4 feet x 4 feet (1.25 x 1.25 m). This size maintains consistent and even moisture at the core of the pile, which is important because water is the key to maintaining the process of decomposition. Moisture is needed for soil microbes to work, multiply, and be happy. Set the pile on the ground or on wood boards. You want to allow earthworms and decay-focused insects to easily access your compost piles. The pile should be at least 4 feet (1.25 m) high, but not so tall that you can't easily add organic materials to it.

Compost piles can be placed anywhere. Areas with more shade will help maintain moisture in the pile, which means less watering will be needed. Place a tarp over the pile to maintain moisture if you feel your pile is drying out too quickly in the summer sun.

You can simply make piles of organic matter on your property for composting. However, you may want to construct a basic compost pen or bin to keep your compost contained. To make a low-cost pen, follow the same dimensions and use chicken wire or metal fencing and four posts to build the sides. The pen should be designed to easily open in the front. We like pens because they stop the wind from blowing lighter materials, like leaves, off the pile.

We recommend not putting a permanent cover over the pen, as you want to encourage the pile to absorb rain. These pictures of Gary's composting pens can be used as examples. The next step is to fill the pen with organic refuse.

You can use anything natural that decays to build the pile. Fill it with spent vegetable plants, weeds, leaves, kitchen food scraps, old potting soil, bed edgings, and grass cuttings. If you use fresh-cut grass, only add 1 or 2 bags weekly and mix it gently into the top of the pile with other debris. Grass can begin to smell as it decays if the layer of grass is too thick. However, it does not cause harm to the pile. Fill the pen as quickly as possible to reach that minimum height. The pile's height will drop as the decomposition process starts. Keep adding to the pile over the growing season. It will take, in general, 1 to 2 years to get a good quantity of completed compost using the cold composting method. After that, you can harvest compost yearly by simply keeping the pen filled with fresh organic matter season to season. Completed compost is harvested from the bottom of the pile. Not only do you get wonderful compost, you also get worm castings mixed throughout the compost.

How to Make Leaf Mold

Leaf mold is decomposed leaves. Molds and fungi are more responsible for breaking the leaves down than bacteria, but the result is still composted organic matter. Leaf mold is based on one ingredient only: leaves. If you have trees or can get bagged leaves from a curb, you can make an amazing soil amendment. Earthworms love leaves and thrive in them. Your finished leaf mold will be loaded with worm castings. Simply build a pen with the same dimensions as a general compost pen and fill it with leaves. Soak the leaves as you fill the pen for the first time and soak the pile down as needed. If you don't have room for a pen, use a metal trash can with a dozen large holes drilled in the bottom for drainage and to allow worms to creep up into the bin. You are basically mimicking what happens on a forest floor. Making leaf mold is the easiest way to get started composting, and it's not much more than piling leaves into a pen. It takes about one season for the process to complete. Over

time, the process speeds up because more and more earthworms show up to help out. Just keep the pile moist and in a somewhat shady area, if possible, and let Nature get quietly to work.

Leaf mold is easy to make, and the final product is perfect for maintaining planting areas.

Don't delay making your own compost! A simple pile works just as well as a fancy bin.

MAKING AN ALL-PURPOSE OUTDOOR PLANTING MIX TO FILL PLANTING BEDS

There is nothing wrong with buying pre-bagged soil mixes except for the expense and the confusion often associated with how they are labeled. Bagged products are primarily made with peat moss. The more peat moss they contain, the more expensive they become. Bags that are labeled garden soil, raised bed mix, container mix, or potting mix essentially vary in the amount of peat moss they have. They contain very little compost and sometimes a bit of fertilizer. The most cost-effective way to fill your containers and garden beds is to make your own all-purpose planting mix. It will be as good as the bagged products, if not better. Amendments like fertilizer and compost can be added at your discretion.

We recommend starting with this simple 50/50 base mix for filling containers and garden beds and amending planting holes. Start with 50 percent peat moss. Peat moss may not be available in your area, or you may want to substitute it for ecological reasons. Finely milled coco coir can be used as a substitute. Where neither of these products are available, or if you choose not to use them, compost can be used instead. Peat moss and coco coir do not contain much in the way of nutrition for the plants or soil microbes. They are used to help create a loose growing medium, and they hold moisture well.

To finish your base mix, add 50 percent of the native earth from your yard. It can be any quality. If you don't have land, you can use the less expensive bagged topsoil products from stores.

If you purchase a bale of compressed peat moss and bags of lower-priced topsoil from garden centers, you can blend them together as your 50/50 base mix and make something that looks like the premium bagged soil products they are also selling. Buying bulk ingredients and blending is the second-cheapest way to make soil mixes. The first is using your own homemade compost and earth.

Once you have the 50/50 base mix, you can add to it as you wish, using amendments you may have or be willing to purchase. We make this type of base mix and amend it as needed based on what we are growing or filling. Fully composted organic matter, as discussed, is the best amendment for your garden plants and beds. A good guideline that can be adjusted at your discretion is ⅔ of the base mix and ⅓ compost. Making your own compost helps to keep your edible landscape sustainable when it comes to plant nutrient needs, soil needs, and budget needs. The above mix ratios are effective, but in a perfect world, 50 percent compost and 50 percent native soil is all you need for your gardens.

Budget Saver #6: Order Truckloads of Compost and Soil Locally

We understand that not everyone has the land to compost or the time to make their own soil mixes. A great alternative to making your own or buying it in the form of expensive bagged products is to shop locally. Local farms and landscape companies often make compost, garden soil, and mulch. Your local municipality may make compost or even make leaf mold as Gary's does. Buying yards of material is a cheaper alternative to bagged products when building a lot of new planting areas. Many places allow you to inspect their products, and you can order yards of compost, garden soil, and mulch as needed for delivery. Gary did this several times over the first couple of years when he was building the beds for his edible landscape. Ask neighbors and do some research until you find a company you really like. It is a cheaper and more convenient alternative to lugging bagged products from stores to your garden.

SEED STARTING AND GROWING TRANSPLANTS

The least expensive way to get plants for your edible landscape is through starting seeds and growing transplants. Trees, fruit canes, and bushes often have to be purchased from a nursery or ordered online. This can be expensive. To offset the cost of these additions to your gardens, many edible plants can be started indoors from seed. Winter and early spring are often too cold to direct-sow seeds outdoors in many areas. You can get a jump on the season by starting them in your home under grow lights. A basic setup of inexpensive white LED shop lights, a shelf, seed-starting trays, a small box of water-soluble fertilizer, and seed-starting potting mix is all that is needed to grow herb, flower, fruit, and vegetable transplants indoors. You can grow 6- to 12-week-old transplants inside while waiting for spring to show up. Detailed instructions on starting plants indoors are beyond the scope of this book, but the following sections are enough to get you started.

Gary starts perennial herbs indoors for groundcover and filling pockets in his edible landscape.

Grow Lights and Shelving

A general rule of thumb is to have your grow lights on for 14 hours and off for 10 hours. Many plants do need a period of darkness. A sunny window will not work for starting seeds indoors. You can purchase very expensive grow lights or you can look for basic white LED shop lights. Gary has used these types of lights for 10 years with great success. The shop light should be 4 feet (1.2 m) long, which is standard, and it should have 2 rows of lights under the hood. Shop lights should have plugs on them for wall outlets and not be set up to be hardwired into a ceiling outlet. One of the two ratings you want on the lights is 5,000 Kelvin or higher. That rating mimics daylight the best. The other rating is 5,000 lumens or higher for the intensity of the light, or brightness. The lights should sit 2 or 3 inches (5 to 7.5 cm) above the starting mix at planting. After the seeds germinate and have grown for 2 to 3 weeks, the lights can be raised to sit 4 to 6 inches (10 to 15 cm) above the leaves. The height does vary slightly based on what is being grown and how bright your lights are rated. When in doubt, keep the light closer to the plants and adjust upward if the light seems to damage the leaves. We recommend getting a shelf with at least four tiers to manage your space as a plant-growing station. The shelves should be wide enough to hold the lights lengthwise. Gary's growing station uses two lights per shelf, but you can start with one light and expand as needed.

Seed-Starting Mixes and Container Preparation

Seeds should be started in a sterile seed-starting mix. The best way to do this is to hydrate any mix you purchase with boiling water before using it. Soil life is not needed at this point for germination and initial growth. There is no need to worry about boiling water damaging the mix. Most seed-starting mixes are soilless and consist of a peat moss, vermiculite, and perlite base. They don't have any beneficial microbes in them. Once planted outdoors, the transplants will enjoy the living soil and thrive. However, there is a significant risk to getting fungus gnats when using these peat-based seed-starting mixes, as their eggs often lie dormant in the mix. The boiling water will kill the eggs. Gary puts his planting medium in a tote and adds enough boiling

water to fully saturate the mix. He typically does this 2 or 3 days before planting his seeds to give the mix some time to dry in case he accidently oversaturates it. Purchase any seed-starting mix that comes in a sealed bag. Do not use outdoor soil amendments, outdoor soil, or starting mix that has been opened and left outside, or you run the risk of bringing in insects, fungi, and other potential problems.

Once the seed-starting mix is hydrated and cooled, it is ready to be used. Add the starting mix to your containers and firm it slightly, but don't over-pack or press it into the containers. You can use standard seed-starting cells, washed and repurposed yogurt cups, cut water bottles, or any small container you want to repurpose for growing transplants. All seed-starting containers must have drainage holes. Plant root systems should not sit in standing water or the roots will rot.

Starting Seeds Indoors

Starting seeds indoors is budget friendly, and it allows you to source different edible plants from across the globe. Purchasing seeds to either start indoors or direct sow opens your landscape to thousands of edible plant varieties that you just won't find locally. A favorite winter activity of ours is searching the internet and garden groups for edible plants we have never grown. There is no need to confine yourself and your garden to the "same old, same old" seeds you see in every store. Explore the world and fill your edible landscape with something unique and exciting. The main reason to start seeds indoors during late winter and early spring is to get the plants to transplant size before planting them out in the garden. When conditions finally become right, you are ahead of the game. Growing

seasons vary from short to long. Transplants help plants grow to maturity in gardens that have shorter seasons, and they help bring food to our tables more quickly when planted in any garden.

The bottom line is that most seeds will germinate as long as they have moisture and are planted with temperatures generally between 65°F to 75°F (18°C to 24°C). This is a fair temperature range for most homes. If temperatures are lower, seeds may take longer to germinate. Very fine seeds like oregano, thyme, or snapdragons should be lightly sprinkled on the starting mix and gently rubbed into and pressed onto the surface of the starting mix. Larger seeds like tomato or pepper seeds should be planted ¼ inch (1 cm) below the surface and covered lightly with the mix. Larger seeds like peas, beans, and squash can be planted ½ to 1 inch (1.5 to 2.5 cm) deep. Don't worry too much about the exact depth; just use seed size as a basic guideline for depth. Some seeds may require special care, and you will find that noted on their seed package.

Plants will vary in the amount of time they should be grown indoors based on how slowly they mature. To help simplify starting times, use the charts below for starting some of the more common edible plants. The seed package often recommends a time frame for starting the seeds indoors. Use your last average frost date as a guide to when you should start your plants indoors. Some plants can take a light frost and can be planted before the last frost date. Others are frost sensitive and should be planted several weeks past the last frost date. Each plant variety can be researched online to find out if it is frost sensitive and when it likes to be transplanted into the ground. This is where your temperature data chart, described in chapter 4, comes in handy.

SEED-STARTING GUIDE FOR HERBS

Herbs	*When to Start Seeds Indoors	Planting Depth	Seed-Starting Tips
Chives *Allium schoenoprasum*	10–12 weeks	Just below the surface.	Plant 6 to 8 seeds per cell.
Lavender *Lavandula angustifolia*	12 weeks	Just below the surface.	Refrigerate seeds for 14 days before planting to help with germination. Plant 4 seeds per cell.
Oregano *Origanum vulgare*	10–12 weeks	Press onto the surface.	Sprinkle 10–20 seeds on the surface and press them in. Divide seedlings later.
Parsley *Petroselinum crispum*	6–8 weeks	¼ inch (1 cm) deep.	Plant 4–6 seeds per cell.
Rosemary *Salvia rosmarinus*	12 weeks	Just below the surface.	Refrigerate seeds for 14 days before planting to help with germination. Plant 4 seeds per cell.
Sage *Salvia officinalis*	8–10 weeks	¼ inch (1 cm) deep.	Plant 4–6 seeds per cell.
Thyme *Thymus vulgaris*	10–12 weeks	Press onto the surface.	Sprinkle 10–20 seeds on the surface and press them in. Divide seedlings later.

*Start your plants indoors by identifying the average last frost date in your area and count backward by the recommended time frame for a starting date.

SEED-STARTING GUIDE FOR EDIBLE FLOWERS

Edible Flowers	*When to Start Seeds Indoors	Planting Depth	Seed-Starting Tips
Borage *Borago officinalis*	4 weeks	¼ inch (1 cm) deep.	Plant 3 seeds per cell and thin to 1 plant.
Calendula *Calendula officinalis*	6–8 weeks	¼ inch (1 cm) deep.	Plant 3 seeds per cell and thin to 2 plants.
Chamomile *Matricaria chamomilla*	4–6 weeks	Press onto the surface.	Sprinkle 10–20 seeds on the surface and press them in. Divide seedlings later.
Echinacea *Echinacea purpurea*	10 weeks	¼ inch (1 cm) deep.	Plant 4–6 seeds per cell and divide seedlings later.
Nasturtium *Tropaeolum majus*	4–6 weeks	½ inch (1.5 cm) deep.	Soak seeds overnight before starting them. Plant 1 seed per cell.
Pansy *Viola x wittrockiana*	10 weeks	¼ inch (1 cm) deep. **Plant below the surface.	Can take 4 weeks to germinate. Plant 6–8 seeds per cell.

*Start your plants indoors by identifying the average last frost date in your area and count backward by the recommended time frame for a starting date.
**Pansy seeds are very small and require darkness to germinate. Lightly pressing the seed into the soil is beneficial so that seed comes in contact with the soil. They should then be covered with black plastic.

SEED-STARTING GUIDE FOR VEGETABLES

Vegetables	*When to Start Seeds Indoors	Planting Depth	Seed-Starting Tips
Arugula *Eruca vesicaria*	2–4 weeks	Just below the surface.	Plant 3–4 seeds per cell. Do not thin.
Lettuce *Lactuca sativa*	6 weeks	¼ inch (1 cm) deep.	Plant 3 seeds per cell and thin to the strongest plant.
Mustard Greens *Brassica juncea*	4 weeks	¼ inch (1 cm) deep.	Plant 2–3 seeds per cell and thin to the strongest.
Peas *Pisum sativum*	3–4 weeks	½ inch (1.5 cm) deep.	Plant 1 seed per cell.
**Peppers *Capsicum* spp.	10–12 weeks	¼ inch (1 cm) deep.	Plant 2 seeds per cell and thin to the strongest.
Spinach *Spinacia oleracea*	6–8 weeks	¼ inch (1 cm) deep.	Plant 2 seeds per cell and do not thin.
Tomatoes *Solanum lycopersicum*	6–8 weeks	¼ inch (1 cm) deep.	Plant 2 seeds per cell and thin to the strongest.

*Start your plants indoors by identifying the average last frost date in your area and count backward by the recommended time frame for a starting date.
**Peppers can take up to 4 weeks to germinate. Super-hot pepper varieties tend to take a longer time to germinate.

These pea seeds have recently sprouted indoors. They'll be transplanted out into the garden within a few days.

Bottom watering is the most effective way to water seed starts indoors. Fill the tray with water and allow the soil to absorb the water from below. Wait 30 minutes, then pour off the excess water.

Watering Seed Starts

All growing containers should be placed in a plastic seed-starting tray or flat. A foil baking tray can be used as an alternative to standard nursery flats. The trays make it easier to move your seed starts and transplants around. The trays are also used to water the plants from the bottom. The planting medium will wick the water upward through the holes in the bottom of the growing containers. All mixes will turn dark brown when fully saturated, and they dry from the top of the container downward. When the top of the starting mix has turned a light brown and is uniformly dry, it is time to water them again, likely a few days later. It is important to let the surface dry and stay dry for a couple of days. This helps to reduce fungi, mold, and algae growth. The required frequency of watering depends on several factors, but plant size is the biggest factor. The larger the plants and root systems become, the more frequently watering will need to occur.

Watering from above can splash out seeds and soil and splash around potential diseases if present. Also, it is much more time consuming. Bottom watering is more sterile, less time consuming, and easier overall. Simply fill the tray with water to a depth of ¼ to ⅓ of the tray. Allow the growing containers about 30 minutes to sit in the water.

After 30 minutes, the top of the starting mix should be dark brown and saturated. If there is water left in the trays, it should be dumped out. With time and practice, you'll figure out how much water to use so you don't have excess.

Keep young seedlings and transplants regularly watered. Do not allow them to dry out repeatedly.

Community Ecology Institute team member Erica Jones talks with a community member about how to care for a young plant they are about to take home from Freetown Farm.

Fertilizing Seed Starts

Germination may occur within a week, or it may take four weeks or longer, depending on what you are growing. Germination times can vary greatly across seed varieties. General information about germination time is found on the seed package. Once germination occurs, the seedling lives off the nutrients found in its endosperm to start. We recommend fertilizing your seedlings beginning at 7 days after germination with a very diluted organic water-soluble fertilizer. Most fertilizers are meant for outdoor use, so use them at ¼ strength of the recommended dose. You only need small traces of nitrogen, phosphorus, and potassium when growing in very little starting mix, and adding too many nutrients can cause damage. When it is time to water your transplants, add fertilizer to the water. After the first feeding, feed your seedlings every 7 to 14 days thereafter with diluted fertilizer.

Many seeds can also be directly sown into garden beds when soil temperatures and conditions become optimal. While we wait for this time, we can grow other plants indoors. Remember the benefit to starting seeds indoors is to have transplants ready to go. This helps us get plants to size more quickly once placed outdoors. With experience, you will learn the best ways to plant your gardens. The only way to learn is to have fun, experiment, and get your hands dirty.

Chiara in the green house with seed starts.

Indoor Transplants Need to Be Acclimated to the Outdoors

Seedlings grown indoors have not been exposed to the sun, the wind, or temperatures above or below the coziness of the house. They must be slowly acclimated to the outdoor elements in order to build up a tolerance to these fluctuations. Plants moved outside without being properly acclimated may get sunburned and can die.

Transplants should be acclimated over a 10-day period. There is no set way to do this other than to do it slowly. Weather varies greatly, but this method will get you started. Day 1 of acclimation, on a fully sunny day, the plants should be placed outdoors for 20 to 30 minutes. If it is overcast, the plants can stay outdoors for 60 to 90 minutes. We recommend using the morning sun to acclimate plants. Start with 30 minutes outdoors on day 1 and day 2. Transplants can be left outdoors for 60 minutes on days 3 and 4. On days 5, 6, and 7, plants can stay outside for 90 minutes. After the first week, Gary leaves his plants outdoors during the day but brings them inside at night. He likes to keep them outside where they only get morning sun and shade thereafter, which is typically the east side of his house. Bring your plants in if it is going to rain and don't place them where they can bake in the afternoon sun. The last thing you want to do is spend months growing beautiful transplants only to rush them outdoors to be harmed by the sun, wind, and harsh temperature changes.

Chop and Drop

Plants higher in nitrogen are often grown in beds and chopped to be left to decay where they lie. That can be difficult to do in beds that have plants actively growing. Chop and drop can also refer to removing plant material from around one's property during the season, cutting it into pieces, and dropping it right onto the soil where you have plants growing. This strategy is aimed at garden fertilization, and it benefits soil life, adds nitrogen to the soil (the percentage is based on what you are chopping and dropping), provides an organic mulch that prevents water evaporation, moderates soil temperature, and minimizes erosion. This method can be used for large parts of the garden as part of your composting plans by simply letting plant materials decompose where they are placed. You can do this with just about any plant that hasn't produced mature seeds that you want to avoid spreading. You can also intentionally grow cover crops like comfrey and crimson clover. They can be cut down and allowed to decay where they fall, enriching future planting beds, or the clippings can be moved to other growing beds to decay.

Weeding and Mulching

Once your beds are established and planted, the less exciting chore of weeding always follows and unfortunately stays on our to-do lists week after week. Weeds will always show up. It is worth identifying your local weeds as they are often edible in some capacity. Our favorite example is the dandelion, which is fully detailed in chapter 5. We use the leaves all the time in our spring salads. Yes, one way to deal with weeds is to eat them, but there are two other very effective ways to manage weeds and reduce the need for heavy weeding. The first is to not turn your soil once your beds are established, and the second is to use mulch. A lot of weed seeds lie dormant below the soil surface, and it is not until the soil is turned and the seeds are brought closer to the surface that they germinate. Continued soil turning means more weeds.

Mulch provides many benefits to garden beds. We recommend using 2 to 3 inches (5 to 8 cm) of mulch in the spring to control weeds and provide other benefits to our gardens through the growing season. Mulching reduces the frequency of manual watering, it maintains moisture evenly throughout the depth of the soil, it keeps soil cooler during the high heat of summer, it helps soil stay warmer when the cold nights roll in, and it provides organic matter to earthworms, soil microbes, and other garden life. Weeds that grow in the mulch over the season are very easily pulled out and managed. Gary recommends composting all your weeds using the cold composting method discussed earlier. The best way to manage weeds in your landscape is to walk around your property weekly and pull weeds as they appear. Some weeds have deep taproots. They are best managed early on, before the root grows deeply into the ground. Very often, any piece of root left behind is enough for the weed to reestablish and reappear. Weeding is an ongoing chore that is best managed through routine.

Ongoing Care and Maintenance

A comprehensive tending and care guide is impossible to provide because climate, soil, plant species, and gardening methods vary so greatly. But composting and fertilizing, watering, inspecting plants for pests and diseases, and mulching are standard care activities in most gardens. For example, we add compost to our garden beds when the growing season ends in the late fall, or we add it in the early spring several weeks before we begin planting the beds. Sometimes we compost the beds at both times, if we're growing plants that feed heavily. Gary calls these times "putting beds to rest for winter slumber" and "waking them up for spring growing." Each piece of your edible landscape will require different care. The best way to care for your trees, bushes, canes, vines, and plants is to set up a garden routine similar to the table below. Use this as a general template and adapt it to the unique needs of your edible landscape.

GARDEN CARE & MAINTENANCE GUIDELINES

Compost your growing beds at least once at the end of the season or at the start of spring.	Use 1 to 2 inches (2.5–5 cm) of composted organic matter, composted manure, or composted leaves, or a combination of any of the three.
Compost your growing bed in the middle of the growing season.	For a top-dressing and midseason boost, use 1 inch (2.5 cm) of compost. Simply scatter it onto the surface of the growing beds around the trees, bushes, and other plants.
Add slow-release organic granular fertilizer to each planting hole as needed.	Use 1 to 2 tablespoons (14 to 29 g) of organic granular fertilizer that has nitrogen, phosphorus, and potassium represented; mix well in the planting hole for any new annual plants. Use 1 handful for established large plants such as trees, bushes, fruit canes, vines, or any other perennial plant. Scatter it across the soil surface.
A water-soluble fertilizer should be used to water-in new transplants as needed.	A quick soaking of the root area is all that is needed to help the new plants establish. A quick feed to perennial plants will help them get off to a good start.
Mulch beds in the spring that are not being used for directly sowing seeds.	Use 2 to 3 inches (5–8 cm) of mulch in the spring for beds with established plants. Other garden beds with new plants can be mulched when the plants are about 8 inches (20 cm) tall. Never mulch over newly planted seeds, and don't try to grow seeds in mulch—they should be planted directly in the soil.
Anything that is newly planted or directly seeded should be watered regularly.	Watering will vary based on temperatures. To establish new plants, water them every other day for the first week and every third day for another week. Pick a routine that best works in your area.
Water established beds a minimum of two times weekly.	With mixed planting beds it is not practical to focus on different moisture needs of plants. Entire beds should be watered twice a week. A heavy soaking rain can replace hand watering. As summer heat arrives, an additional watering day should be added as needed. The beds should be watered so, at minimum, the top 6 inches (15 cm) of soil is thoroughly soaked.
Inspect plants for signs of pests and diseases at least one time a week.	Check plant leaves for signs of pests and disease with diligence and regularity. The best way to prevent problems and manage them is to discover and treat them early. We do this at least twice a week.

There is always more to do when it comes to tending and maintaining gardens. This table covers the essential tasks and chores needed to care for an edible landscape. Over time and with experience, these tasks will become easier to manage. There is no need to worry too much about care. Set up a routine and structure that fits into your daily life. Take time to enjoy the beauty of your garden, do your best, and make adjustments as needed. You can always move plants around and balance your edible landscape a little more each year.

Our passions for nature and gardens shaped our journey. Our path has led to teaching and building programs in our community. The next chapter offers a little insight into where our paths have gone. Perhaps your journey may lead there too.

8

CHANGING THE LANDSCAPE AND CULTIVATING COMMUNITY

The primary goal of this book is to help you learn how to see the land where you and your family live, learn, work, and play through new eyes. The big question is how can the land we have access to be transformed into a beautiful, abundant space that feeds both our stomachs and our spirits while also supporting the health of the natural environment? Starting with the land right outside your door, what steps can you take to start growing something delicious that brings you joy? This could be colorful pots filled with herbs on a sunny patio. It could be a small rectangle of shade-happy native plants that support local pollinators and offer tasty contributions to a salad or stir-fry. It could be a more classic vegetable garden camouflaged and/or accentuated by edible flowers. It could be a small food forest on the perimeter of your yard. The key is to start somewhere where you are in charge and use that space to hone your knowledge of how to grow a variety of edible plants.

Left: Growing an edible landscape right in your front yard is a wonderful way to build community-wide interest in food gardening.

Community Ecology Institute (CEI) community photo taken in the summer of 2022 after NBC came to Freetown Farm to film our work for *The Today Show*.

Here, CEI families are outside a community native tree grove they planted and tend each year.

It is likely that people who see your gardening efforts will offer you compliments and ask you questions. Gardening and creating beauty are natural door-openers to conversations in a community. People will want to learn about what you are doing and, if they are gardeners too, offer you stories or ideas that bring them joy. Consider inviting your neighbors over to lend a hand with a gardening project, or bring them some of your harvest so they can appreciate your gardening. We suggest asking your neighbors which things they enjoy eating fresh and seeing if you can collaborate on gardening along shared fences (or take some boundaries down and create common space to grow in).

After you have momentum in your own yard and neighborhood, expand your horizons to think about other places that would benefit from a small community-tended garden. This is an opportunity to find common ground with new people. It will create opportunities for learning and growing together and will help others connect over the well-being created by harvesting and sharing food together. Once you create your first garden in the community, you will likely see opportunities for new gardens all over the place.

We came to write this book together through our shared work with the Community Ecology Institute at Freetown Farm. Through this work, we have seen just how much good comes from connecting with the community to help people from all walks of life learn how to grow and share food where they live, learn, work, and play. Founded in 2016, the Community Ecology Institute (CEI) is a non-profit organization with a mission to cultivate communities where people and nature thrive together. CEI focuses on tangible, community-level change at the intersection of environment, education, equity, and health. Our experiential education programs concentrate on four Cs: Connection to Nature, Civic Ecology, Community Health, and Climate Action. We showcase and teach evidence-based best practices in these areas that are specifically responsive to Howard County's natural and social ecosystems. We also develop resources for other communities to help them engage the people they serve in nature-based opportunities that enhance community well-being.

FREETOWN FARM

In the summer of 2019, CEI purchased a small farm in the city of Columbia, Maryland, to protect it from housing development and make it accessible to the community. With tremendous community support, we became the new stewards of the last working farm in our hometown. Since then, the CEI team has transformed the once-dormant property into an inviting place where community members can learn through hands-on experience about ways to lead happier, healthier, more connected, sustainable lives. As the stewards of this land, CEI has begun to significantly expand both the types of programs we offer and the populations we serve, working with other organizations to donate fresh food to people in need while providing volunteers with meaningful community connections.

Before and after photos of the back half of Freetown Farm.

Rainbow of veggies harvested from the farm.

Gardening cohorts at work in the food forest.

Zaneta and other Nourishing Gardens team members helping to plant the bio-retention pond at Freetown Farm with native species.

Freetown Farm is now a vibrant place of common ground for diverse members of our community. It showcases more than a dozen different growing areas that demonstrate how people can transform the land where they live in ways that are beautiful and good for the natural environment, not to mention full of delicious food!

NOURISHING GARDENS

In 2021 we created our Nourishing Gardens program, which seeks to transform lawns into edible, ecologically beneficial gardens while providing experiential learning and workforce-development opportunities. The program brings the benefits, learning, and experience of Freetown Farm directly to the front doors of our neighbors. At the start of the program, the Nourishing Gardens team worked at Freetown Farm to add trees and shrubs to a food forest, plant fall crops in the market garden, and plant native, pollinator-supporting plant species around our new bio-retention pond. Trainees then applied their experience to community-based installations, expanding CEI's impact beyond the farm. These installations included planting gardens at local schools and in city-owned open space, as well as a publicly accessible food garden at a community college.

The Grow It, Eat It Garden mural at Freetown Farm

A colorful entrance to the Grow It, Eat It garden and greenhouse.

CEI team members, Peter and Simon, with a colorful harvest from Freetown Farm.

School installations are some of our favorite jobs to participate in.

In 2022, trainees installed 23 gardens throughout our community, providing growing space to more than 50,000 community members who might not otherwise have land to grow on. More than 500 community members were involved in garden planning, installation, and care, and more than 1,300 food and pollinator plants were planted, adding to the biodiversity of our ecosystem. At the close of the year, five of our Nourishing Gardens trainees were offered opportunities to earn an income from CEI, fulfilling our wish to provide meaningful green infrastructure jobs in our community.

A NAACP group outside of their garden at Freetown Farm.

Some of the Nourishing Gardens team at Freetown Farm.

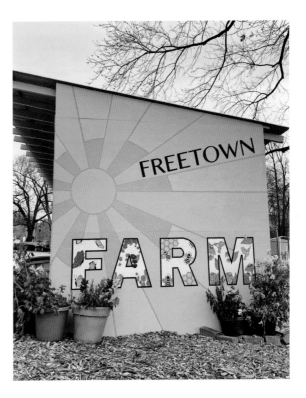

CONCLUSION

Our individual passions for gardening and love for nature led us down a path to writing this book and developing the programs we mentioned. As you transform your space from less lawn to something amazing, take a step back and appreciate what you created in the earth. We hope you find joy and peace watching new varieties of plants grow and watching wildlife fill your edible landscape. Most of all, we hope you get to share your passion, as we have, with family, friends, and neighbors. Growing and harvesting food is something that human beings have done from nearly the beginning of our time. Our knowledge of how to do this has fallen into a slumber over the years. You are one of many that are waking up to the idea that we can grow our own food and that it is something to be proud of. As you tend your gardens and harvest food, consider building programs that will share your passion in your community. In the same way that nature touches you, you will pass those feelings on to someone you haven't met yet. We believe that is a good thing.

Right: Growing an edible landscape is a never-ending journey. Welcome!

RESOURCES

Books

- *The Joy of Foraging* by Gary Lincoff
- *Food Not Lawns: How to Turn Your Yard into a Garden and Your Neighborhood into a Community* by H.C. Flores
- *Growing Perennial Foods: A Field Guide to Raising Resilient Herbs, Fruits, and Vegetables* by Acadia Tucker
- *The Modern Homestead Garden: Growing Self-Sufficiency in Any Size Backyard* by Gary Pilarchik
- *The Backyard Homestead: Produce All the Food You Need on Just a Quarter Acre!* by Carleen Madigan
- *Edible Landscaping with a Permaculture Twist: How to Have Your Yard and Eat It Too* by Michael Judd
- *Rambunctious Garden: Saving Nature in a Post-Wild World* by Emma Marris
- *The Edible Front Yard: The Mow-Less, Grow-More Plan for a Beautiful, Bountiful Garden* by Ivette Soler
- *Edible Landscaping: Now You Can Have Your Gorgeous Garden and Eat It Too!* by Rosalind Creasy

Websites

- The Community Ecology Institute: www.communityecologyinstitute.org
    - Community of Families in Nature (CFIN)
    - Freetown Farm
    - Nourishing Gardens

- The Rusted Garden Vegetable Seeds & Home Garden Supplies www.therustedgarden.com

- Grow Food Not Lawns www.foodnotlawns.com

- Permaculture Institute, Inc. https://permaculture.org

ABOUT THE AUTHORS

Dr. Chiara D'Amore is the Founder and Executive Director of the Community Ecology Institute, a non-profit organization working to cultivate communities in which people and nature thrive together. She holds a PhD in Sustainability Education and an MS in Environmental Science and Engineering. She is an adjunct faculty at Prescott College, where she teaches courses related to climate change, civic ecology, experiential education, and research design. She worked as an environmental consultant for over 15 years, serving clients such as the United Nations, the U.S. Environmental Protection Agency, and numerous energy utilities. Dr. D'Amore's work is focused on fostering environmental and social well-being by reconnecting people with the natural environment as well as designing, implementing, and evaluating environmental and educational programs. As a mother, educator, community-builder, activist, artist, writer, and scholar, she is dedicated to helping people of all ages and backgrounds to lead happier, healthier, more connected, sustainable lives. Learn more at www.chiaradamore.com.

Gary Pilarchik is the content creator and owner of The Rusted Garden. He is a retired licensed clinical social worker and has joyfully moved toward teaching people how to garden as his full-time job. He learned how to grow plants from his grandfather while in grade school, and the passion has only gotten stronger. This is his second book. His first book, *The Modern Homestead Garden: Growing Self-Sufficiency in Any Size Backyard*, was published in 2020. He became a board member of The Community Ecology Institute in 2020, and he volunteers at one of the non-profit initiatives, Freetown Farm. He lives in an 1867 farmhouse with his wife, Angela, and has turned his two acres (0.8 ha) into an edible landscape over the last five years. He hopes to spread his passion for nature and growing food to others. You can find him under The Rusted Garden on YouTube (over 700,000 subscribers) and on Instagram (over 100,000 followers). He has made over 2,000 gardening videos, all focused on helping people have a more successful garden. He truly believes it when he says, "A garden wants to give; all we have to do is help it along." You can support his work by following him on social media and visiting his seed and garden shop at www.therustedgarden.com.

AUTHOR ACKNOWLEDGMENTS

Chiara:

- Thank you to Gary for the opportunity to co-write this book. It has been a joy to learn and grow with you, and I am so grateful for all the time and talent you have shared with Freetown Farm.
- Thank you to all the wonderful people who contribute to the Community Ecology Institute and have helped make it such an inspiring journey to share. A special thank you to Erica Jones, Theresa Taylor, and Christy Ferguson (and Gary!) for all your work on creating the Nourishing Gardens program, and to Jean Silver-Isenstadt for your mentorship and leadership.
- Thank you to Madison Townsend for help with researching the details of some of the plants featured in this book, and to Edwin Gould, Kim Glinka, and Sofi Fedushchenko for sharing their gardening journeys and photos.
- Thank you to my family for all of your love and support. Bryce and Sasha, I love you to the moon and back.

Gary:

- Thanks to Jeff for helping me build the supports needed to maintain The Rusted Garden
- To my family—Angela, Jenna, Alec, Willow, Tucker, and Nova—thanks for making the homestead a special place to gather.
- Thanks to Chiara for creating a place that welcomes the world. I am glad we crossed paths.
- I am grateful for the kindness shown by all the gardeners I have encountered through my journey with The Rusted Garden, which began over a decade ago.

PHOTO CREDITS

CEI Team: page 86

Trina Dalziel: pages 71, 81, 84, 88

Chiara D'Amore: pages 29 (right), 34, 35 (top), 35 (bottom), 36, 37, 38 (bottom), 66 (right), 68, 82, 83, 92 (top), 101 (bottom), 111 (top right), 111 (bottom left), 113 (bottom left), 118, 124, 126, 141 (right middle), 145 (bottom right), 169 (bottom), 170 (bottom), 176 (left), 176 (right), 177, 178, 179 (bottom), 180 (bottom two), 181 (top), 181 (bottom right)

Christy Ferguson: page 148

Kim Glinka: pages 46, 47, 48, 49, 50, 51, 52, 53

Edwin Gould: pages 40 (top), 40 (bottom), 41

Keri Isenstadt: pages 170 (top), 179 (top)

Angela Pilarchik: page 10

Gary Pilarchik: pages 6, 14, 17, 29 (left), 30, 54, 56 (top), 57, 58, 59, 61, 67, 69, 74, 75, 76, 77, 78, 87, 89, 91, 93 (right), 93 (left), 96, 101 (top), 107 (bottom left), 111 (top left), 112 (top right), 112 (top left), 135, 142 (top), 142 (bottom), 145 (bottom left), 146, 147, 149, 150 (bottom left), 150 (top), 150 (bottom right), 157, 158, 159, 160, 161, 162, 163, 165, 166, 169 (top), 183

Shutterstock: pages 5, 9, 11, 12, 15, 16, 18, 19, 20, 21, 22, 23, 24, 25, 26, 28, 32, 38 (top), 42, 45, 60, 62, 63, 64, 66 (left), 72, 73, 79, 90, 92 (bottom), 94, 98, 100, 102, 104, 107, 108, 110, 111 (bottom right), 112 (bottom), 113 (bottom right), 113 (top), 119, 120, 121, 122, 123, 125, 127, 128, 129, 130, 131, 134, 137, 138, 141, 145 (top), 152, 154, 156, 168, 174

Theresa Taylor: pages 44, 180 (top left), 180 (top right), 181 (bottom left)

Judy White: page 132

INDEX